Hallelujah in the Forest

Richard A. Seaton
and
Dorothy A. Bass

Tapestry Press, Ltd.
Acton, MA

© 1993 by Richard A. Seaton and Dorothy A. Bass.
All rights reserved.

Printed in the United States of America.

ISBN 0-924234-94-6

Contents

Introduction	1
Chapter I— Methodism Meets the Germans	3
Chapter II—Gatherings on the Frontier	9
Chapter III—The Church in the Wildwood	17
Chapter IV—The Cloud of Witnesses	43
Chapter V—The Obedient Ones	55

APPENDICES

List of Pastors of Lake Creek Church	107
Presiding Elders or District Superintendents Who Served Lake Creek from the Beginning	108
Constitution of the Lake Creek Camp Meeting Association	109
Bibliography	111

INTRODUCTION

The history of the Lake Creek Campmeeting cannot be fully understood without a basic understanding of the beginnings of campmeetings in general and also the History of the German Methodist Church. To this end I begin with a short chapter on the History of the German Methodists and then a brief history of the campmeeting movement.

Then we will look at the actual history of the Lake Creek Campmeeting and its development over its 150 years. Another chapter will include actual incidents, that were found in oral history recordings made over the past 20 years, remembering past campmeetings.

The final chapter is the contribution of Dorothy Bass of Smithton who had photographs and so much information on the preachers that have served Lake Creek over the years. I want to say thank you to Eric Page for his research on the subject. Thanks to Becky Rodenbaugh for transcribing a number of the recorded tapes of campmeeting participants. And thank you to the many who have given me material and photographs.

I hope you enjoy this step backward in time as we celebrate the 150th Anniversary of the beginnings of Lake Creek.

Richard A. Seaton

The Tabernacle as it is today at Lake Creek.

Chapter I
METHODISM MEETS THE GERMANS

Long before the German settlers began to come in great numbers to the new world, the German people had a great influence on early Methodism. The German Moravians especially affected John Wesley. The piety and faith of the Moravians that Wesley met en route to Georgia in 1735 caused him to examine his own spiritual state. August Gottleib Spangenberg was a German Moravian Missionary who made Wesley realize the need for a deeper faith. Another Moravian, Peter Bohler, told Wesley how to come into intimate contact with his Savior. When Wesley had his heart warming experience he was listening to the writing of another German, Martin Luther's Preface to the Letter to the Romans.

The early Methodists repaid Wesley's obligation by bringing the Gospel to the new German immigrants. As early as the 1760s German converts were reported under Robert Strawbridge. Bishop Francis Asbury often visited German settlements and since he could not preach in German, Henry Boehm, his traveling companion did the preaching. By 1810 Boehm had preached to Germans in about fourteen different states.

Phillip William Otterbein came to America as a minister of the German Reformed Church, but his evangelistic Methodist style, and his use of the Methodist organizational setup, soon caused the founding of the United Brethren in Christ. Otterbein and Asbury were close friends, and it would seem that the German followers should have become members of the Methodist Episcopal Church. Bishop Asbury was opposed to that. He did not think it would be wise to use two different languages in the Methodist Episcopal Church. He also felt that the German language would soon cease in America and that Methodists should help in the Americanization of the foreigners.

Jacob Albright was the leader of a second Methodist movement among the Germans. He also wanted to bring his followers into the Methodist Episcopal Church but Bishop Asbury kept the same policy and the Evangelical Association was born. These two groups finally united with the Methodists in 1968 forming the United Methodist Church.

Bishop Francis Asbury believed that the German language would die out in America within 15 years, however 15 years after his death an event began that he had not foreseen. In the 1830s the German immigration to America began to assume tremendous proportions. Literally hundreds of thousands of Germans came to America in the next thirty years. Some went to cities such as Cincinnati, Louisville, and St. Louis while others pushed on and settled in the West where land was cheap. Soon, in certain parts of the West, the German Language alone was spoken and newspapers were printed in German and schools were taught by German schoolmasters. The Western Christian Advocate publication began to advocate that work be started among the new German population. This tide of German immigrants needed religious assistance.

It was at this time that William Nast, who has often been called the "Father of German Methodism," comes into the picture. He was born in Stuttgart, Germany on June 15, 1807. His parents were devout Lutheran. Three of his sisters married Lutheran ministers. At William's confirmation he had a religious experience and, at the close, during a shower of rain, he fell on his knees and prayed for pardon and a new heart. He felt a heart-cheering acceptance from God.

During his University days he was the only one out of a class of 50 people training for the ministry who knew anything of experiential religion. With this influence of his peers and with the rationalistic professors instructing him he became a rationalist himself. In his words, "At the conclusion of my studies, I was thoroughly divorced from evangelical faith, and under a deep sense of unfitness for the ministry of any man who is not a true believer—the result of my former Christian Experience—I voluntarily withdrew from the service of the church and repaid out of my private means, small as they were, the cost of my education, which the state required of those who did not enter into service of the church.

In 1828, on hearing of the need for classical teachers in the United States, he first became a tutor in private homes and then a teacher of German at West Point Military Academy.

Dr. William Nast—
Founder of German Methodism.

In 1832 he encountered several Methodist ministers on their way to a campmeeting on the banks of the Junita river. They invited him to accompany them and it was the first time that he had witnessed an assembly of this kind. There was great power of preaching and the Holy Spirit was evident. He became overwhelmed with guilt, understanding God's love and mercy and yet feeling that his own day of grace was past. He wrote of his burden to a Dr. Fisk whom he heard preach with power. Here is a part of Fisk's answer to Nast: "And who are you, my brother, that claims to have produced a case to hard for an Almighty Savior? Hell might indeed triumph if this were true . . . but thanks be to His name, He has Triumphed."

After three years of this burden of guilt he was finally relieved of this weight on January 17, 1835 at a Methodist Quarterly Meeting in Danville, Ohio. He immediately wanted to tell his fellow Germans of his spiritual happiness. Fourteen days later he was licensed to preach and at the same time recommended for admission to the Ohio Conference. That Fall he was appointed as a missionary to the Germans in Cincinnati.

His first year was not very rewarding and produced only three converts. The Board of Missions voted to pay the first year's salary of $100. This was the uniform salary for a single preacher of that day. The success of the young missionary on the first year seemed too meager; so the Cincinnati work was expanded to a 300 mile circuit centering on Columbus and including 25 preaching places. The next two years were not much better and he was almost of a mind to quit. He was ridiculed and received with scorn by many of his fellow Germans. The German Press of Cincinnati, controlled by the brewers, the atheists, and the Roman Catholics, tried to destroy Nast's work by sarcasm and denunciation. This, however, was unwise. Nast was an excellent writer and well educated and felt especially capable to answer these rationalists since he had been one himself. On January 4, 1839 the publication of *Der Christliche Apologete* was begun.

The first society for German Methodist was organized in 1838 under Nast's leadership in Cincinnati. Thirty members were reported. A second mission began in Pittsburgh and a third in Wheeling, West Virginia where the first German Methodist building was erected in 1840. In 1843 the first German Methodist church building west of the Alleghenies was built in Cincinnati. Nast went on to become a leader in German Methodism through his writings, as a member to General Conferences, preparing a commentary on the scriptures in the German language and in editing a German hymn book. Until 1892 he continued as editor of the *Apologete*. He died on May 16, 1899.

In August of 1841, Bishop Morris appointed Ludwig S. Jacoby, one of Nast's converts, whose biography is contained later in this book, to be a "missionary" in the St. Louis area. There were estimated to be about 15,000 Germans living in St. Louis by that time. When Jacoby, his wife, Amalie Nuelsen, and their new five week old daughter arrived in St. Louis they found that "the immigrants spent Sunday in dancing and card playing and had little to do with what meager religious programs were offered. He founded the Wash Street Methodist Church in 1841 by renting two little rooms from the Presbyterians. On the first Sunday Mrs. Jacoby stated that he might be preaching only to her and empty pews but Jacoby went to the belfry and pulled the rope so long and so hard that soon the room was filled. Many came to mock or laugh and were not there for religion. Among the curious that day was a devout Catholic and his wife, who exclaimed after the service: "This man is no atheist, but a converted preacher. To men of this type alone can the Church be trusted." The word spread and the services were soon well attended. He organized a church of 41 members and they began the building of a small frame building at Fourth and Wash Streets. When this church building was dedicated, hoodlums burned brandy on the cornerstone and placed a jug full of liquor on the spot. Jacoby answered this challenge by leading one of the men involved to Christ during the next year. This church was the first German Methodist Congregation organized West of the Mississippi. It was named Salem but it was not a place of peace. Jacoby was threatened by irate German citizens and his services were often interrupted by rowdies. He and his wife were often insulted by vindictive opponents with hostile taunts and jeers. This church was later known as the Cathedral of German Methodism. From that church in St. Louis was laid the foundation of German

6 Chapter I

Methodism in Missouri. The first expansion began to follow the course of the rivers for that is what the immigrants did. The tide of German immigration was very high now. Between 1840 and 1847, 889,000 new German immigrants came to the United States and many of them came to Missouri.

The first German campmeeting in America was organized in 1839 in Mill Creek Valley near Cincinnati. Lake Creek seems to be the second organized. The Germans took to the campmeeting with enthusiasm. It was to them an outing, an AUSFLUG, with a religious purpose. Lake Creek was one of the first German campmeetings organized, yet within 40 years over 35 German campmeetings were in existence. Today Lake Creek exists as the oldest campmeeting west of the Mississippi.

Some of the early German immigrants in the Lake Creek area were the families of Cord Kahrs, Jacob Timken, Gerhard Ringen and others. They had been somewhat organized by a German Methodist Lay Preacher by the name of Francis Walkenhorst who settled in the area in 1839. He seems to have left the area in about two years and the families named above petitioned Dr. William Nast to send a minister to the Lake Creek area. In 1843, Sebastian Barth was sent to form the Osage Mission. The further history of the Lake Creek Community and congregation will be found later.

**Ludwig Jacoby—
First German preacher
assigned to Missouri.**

The rapid expansion of the German congregations caused the General Conference of 1844 to allow the organization of separate German Districts. By this year the German missions were numbered at 19 with a total of 1,500 members. By the year 1860 the German work was part of nine different Annual Conferences, and so in 1864 The General Conference authorized the formation of German Conferences to deal with the work. Many of the German immigrants had such a meager understanding of English that they could not follow the proceedings of the English Conferences. The size of the work with the Germans was such that the new conferences were necessary. By 1864 there were 18 German Districts with 306 preachers and 26,145 members. Three were organized, the Central German Conference, The Northwest German Conference and the Southwest German Conference of which Missouri was part of the latter.

Out of the attempt to evangelize the Germans of the Western United States came the Methodist Mission to the people in Germany. Converted Germans in America wrote to friends and family back home and told them what Methodism had done for them. As a result, many requests came from Germany that the Methodist Episcopal Church send missionaries back to them. In 1849, Ludwig S. Jacoby went to Germany as the first missionary He began to preach in Bremen and by 1865 there were 4,650 Methodists in Germany.

The thousands of modern day Methodists with Germanic names are a tribute to the great work done by these pioneers.

Harper's Weekly cover in 1877 states that Germans will not be true Americans until they break their ties and use English.

Chapter II
GATHERINGS ON THE FRONTIER

By the middle of the Nineteenth Century when the Lake Creek Campmeeting began, this form of gathering was becoming a major social and religious institution. The first campmeeting was actually started by the Presbyterians but quickly became interdenominational. It all began in Kentucky in the early Nineteenth Century. Around 1796, Christians in both Europe and America were praying for a revival of religion in the world. The answer to that prayer found its beginning in the efforts of a Scots-Irish preacher by the name of James McGready in Logan County Kentucky. His preaching was more Methodist than Presbyterian. He felt the need for revival and also felt the Lord worked best in a crowd. It was three years before the fire of the Holy Spirit really began to fall. In June of 1800 some 500 persons showed up for a Sunday Service at the Red River Church. Emotions were intense and conversions were many. However, this was still not the first Campmeeting for only one man had brought provisions in his wagon. Everyone else had to beg or forage in the surrounding countryside. McGready knew the moment had come and he announced that the last week of July would begin a meeting and people were invited to come, bring their grub and bedding and stay for the duration. The Gasper River church was the setting. The largest and greatest was the next year at Cane Ridge. The following letters will give some insight into the beginnings of this great revival.

Early Methodist Campmeeting.

Extract of a letter dated Lexington, Kentucky, March 8, 1801:
    Dear Brother,
        I am glad to inform you, there is a great revival of religion near this place; 51 have been added to our church since you left us; 62 added to

Bryant's station since the 8th of February . . . I suppose upwards of 220 have been added to that church in all . . . in short it seems that all the churches near this are in a prosperous state. In some it appears like a fire that has been long confined—bursting all its barriers, and spreading with a rapidity that is indescribable—attended only with a still small voice.

By summer the impact and power of the Cainridge Campmeeting was felt all over the area.

Early Methodist Campmeeting.

Extract of a letter dated Lexington, Kentucky, August 10, 1801.
Dear Brother,
I hasten to give you an account of the revival of religion and some of the remarkable circumstances thereof. The nicest pencil could not portray to your imagination the full idea of the meeting that took place at Kainridge in Bourbon County . . . to this general assembly I set off last Friday, and arrived there on Saturday about 10 o'clock; I then began to note some of the most extraordinary particulars. I first proceeded to count the waggons (sic) containing families with their provisions, camp equipage, etc. to the number of 147. . . there was a stage erected in the woods about 100 yards from the meeting house where there were a number of Presbyterian and Methodist ministers; one of the former preaching to as many as could get near enough to hear . . . at the same time another large concourse of people collected about 100 yards in an East direction from the meeting house hearing a Methodist speaker, and about 150 yards in a South course was an assembly of black people hearing the exhortation of the blacks . . . last Sunday it is said there were 8 to 10 thousand in one gathering and at two other congregations, from 18,000 to 25,000 souls.

The power of the emotions released during this first campmeeting would be a sign of many that would follow. The meetings were often accompanied by enthusiastic physical and emotional displays. For many on the frontier it was the way to let off the tension built up on the frontier.

Excerpt of a letter to Rev. Dr. Rippon, January 7, 1802.
> "In this one place the people are greatly agitated: they go to meeting, and will continue in this place all night, exhorting, praying, and singing; sometimes the professors of religion appear in raptures, as if they were ready to take their flight to glory, and distressed souls, lying on the floor crying out for mercy . . . . These people are a mixed multitude, made up of Presbyterians, Methodists, and Baptists, engaged in worship together.

Although the Cainridge Campmeeting was the beginning of the campmeeting movement and was started by the Presbyterians it soon became a Methodist institution. The early development of campmeetings can be traced by turning the pages of Francis Asbury's Journal. He was enthusiastic as he heard results of the work. He stated: "God has given us hundreds in 1800, why not thousands in 1801, yea, why not a million if we had faith?" The bishop referred to the revivals as field fighting or as fishing with a large net. On December 12, 1805 he lists a whole series of campmeetings at which many hundreds professed conversion. In 1806 he notes a campmeeting at Long-Calm in Maryland, held in October, at which five hundred and eighty were converted. In 1806 the preachers of Delaware reported 150 days and nights in the woods and 5,368 converted. In August, 1808 at Deer Creek in Ohio he notes there were 23 traveling and local preachers present at a great campmeeting where there were 125 tents and wagons and over 2,000 people. By the time of Asbury's death in 1816 there were at least 600 Methodist Campmeetings held in various parts of the country. With the interest of the Methodists came also uniform rules and organization. The Methodists led by Asbury were intent that the improprieties of the earlier meetings would be avoided so a campmeeting code was established. Curfew at 10:00 and guards with white peeled wood rods patrolled the early camps.

As early as 1809, Asbury began to urge the permanence of the campmeeting locations. This led to the building of tabernacles and cabins on the grounds. Some elaborate establishments have come of this such as Ocean Grove Camp Grounds in New Jersey.

The campmeeting however was never recognized as an official Methodist institution. The name campmeeting does not appear in the general conference journals of the church nor does it appear in the Methodist Disciplines of those years. An early Methodist Historian, Jesse Lee, describes the situation:

> Indeed, these meetings have never been authorized by the Methodists, either at their General or Annual Conferences. They have been allowed of; but we as a body of people, have never made any rules or regulations about them; we allow our presiding elders and traveling

preachers to appoint them when and where they please, and to conduct them in what manner they think fit.

In other words, Jesse Lee acknowledges that this movement was really a grassroots movement.

Methodist Campmeeting in New York, *Harper's Weekly*, August 29, 1868.

The campmeeting did become a widely used frontier institution, mostly Methodist, yet not officially recognized by the denomination. Several special campmeeting hymnbooks were published but were never officially recognized by the American Methodists since they always have had an official hymnal with the first one prepared by John Wesley himself and authorized by the 1784 organizing conference.

The pattern of the later meetings followed the precedent set at Cane Ridge in having large attendance, in duration, and in drawing crowds from a large territory, although none ever equaled the original.

Although there had been revival type meetings before the development of the campmeeting, there were new and striking elements that added both to the appeal and to the excitement. People of all ages were brought together, both male and female, mostly white but with some black and they were together day and night. The joy of coming together with a large number of people was a great adventure to these frontier people. The earlier gatherings had been for men only. Following the Cane Ridge all day and all night type meeting, the women were welcome on equal terms with the men.

True, the women were separated from the men in services by a rail, a board, or sometimes a fence, but they were not separated in religious experience. They were even allowed to testify about their experiences.

The new social setting brought the feeling of the city to the rural environment. Children would find new playmates and find new games and even discover new ways to get into mischief. Men could brag and talk big when they were not close to the setting of their story. The wives would get a change of setting for their unending work. The young people would get a chance to exchange glances and maybe even touch hands with others in brief encounters. Families lived in remote cabins and suddenly found themselves within a few feet of the next family's tent. If the purpose for gathering had not been religious, it would not have been allowed, for there was to much pleasure to sanction. It became the social gathering of the year and naturally began to draw those not interested in religion. At the Cane Ridge gathering six men and a women were found lying under the preaching stand in postures indicating they did not have the type of religion preached above them. The next evening another couple was caught in the act of adultery. The size of the gatherings drew all sorts of people, including hustlers and riffraff. Attempts were made to police the grounds but what went on outside the edges was no one's business and impossible to control. Some legitimate peddlers would enter the camps, book agents, barbers, and boot blacks found it a great place to make a fast buck. Sometimes the preacher would announce the profession of the convert, for example, one stated: "This man is desiring to pull teeth if any of you need his services." Early campmeeting preachers tell many stories of disruptions by drunks. Although liquor was not officially available, there was usually someone along who provided for the alcohol needs of the gathering.

A campmeeting, frontispiece to B. W. Gorham, Camp Meeting Manual, Boston, 1854.

Northern Methodist B. W. Gorham produced a Campmeeting Manual in 1854. Although camp sites could be in several possible shapes (horseshoe shaped, circular or rectangular) certain elements were always present. There was always an elevated preachers stand. Just in front and sometimes to the sides was the area called the mourners' bench or anxious seat or called by some "the glory pen." It was a distinct area where sinners under conviction were brought to experience conversion. After conversion, many of these would become "convert exhorters" who would stand and give witness to others of their conversion and urge others to follow.

Seats for the audience, where they existed consisted of logs or planks laid on stumps The bark was dressed and the top adzed off to make them as comfortable as possible. This was entirely in keeping with John Wesley's rule concerning church seating: "Let there be no pews, and no backs to the seats."

The Campmeeting Manual suggests the tents or camps be arranged around the meeting area with campfires in front of the tents so as to add light to the evening services. Behind the tents would be the wagons and behind them would be the horses and livestock.

To understand more of the organization of the early campmeetings, let us look at Captain Frederick Marryat from England as he describes a Methodist campmeeting as it looked to a total outsider. From his Diary in America he states:

> The camp was raised upon . . . a piece of table land comprising many acres. In the center was about an acre and a half surrounded by cabins built up of rough boards. The area in the center was fitted up with planks, laid about a foot from the ground as seats. At one end, but not close to the cabins was a raised preachers stand. One was speaking while five or six others sat behind him on benches. There were entrances to this central area by the four corners; the whole of it shaded by vast forest trees which ran up to a height of 50 or more feet before throwing out a branch. On the trunks of these trees were fixed lamps for the evening services.
>
> Outside the area of the rough board cabins were hundreds of tents pitched in every quarter. The cabins and tents were the temporary habitations of those who had come many miles to attend the meeting . . . usually a period of from five to ten days. Some of the tents had mattresses to sleep on and some of them even had bedsteads and chests of drawers. At a further distance out were the wagons and other vehicles which had conveyed the people to the meeting. Hundreds of horses were tethered among the trees and provided with forage. It was a most interesting and beautiful scene.
>
> The major portion of those not in the center area were cooking the dinners. Fires were burning in every direction, pots boiling, chickens roasting, and hams seething. Indeed there appeared to be no want of creature comforts.
>
> A trumpet sounded as in days of yore, as a signal that the service was about to commence, and I went into the area and took my seat. One of the preachers arose and started a hymn which was sung by seven or eight hundred present. After the singing of the hymn he commenced an extensive sermon; it was good sound doctrine, and although Methodism, it was Methodism of the mildest tone . . . .
>
> In front of the pulpit was a space railed off and strewn with straw, which I was told was the anxious seat. On . . . one . . . side sat about twenty young females and on the other a few men; in the center was a bench which some men were kneeling in prayer. Gradually the number increased on both sides.
>
> At last an elderly man gave out with a hymn and others joined. Others began to pray raising hands above their heads . . . all the voices became confused . . . and as the din increased so did their enthusiasm. Every minute the excitement increased and some wrung their hands, some tore their hair and called for mercy.

To me it was a scene of horrible agony and despair. When it was at its height, one of the preachers came in and raising his voice above the tumult asked the Lord to receive these who are repenting and returning.

Most staid Englishmen found it hard to understand the scene Captain Marryat described. The campmeeting was a child of the American frontier. It was an accident and it grew spontaneously out of the conditions of the American West.

Reverend Jacob Lanius describes his visit to an 1835 central Missouri campmeeting in his diary: "Our way led us through an uninhabited desert and we were necessitated to ride until ten o'clock at night before we reached a cabin." The following day they arrived and found "the camps occupied and the people coming in very fast." Rev. Lanius describes the evening service like this: "On Sunday night ... their cries for mercy were hideous and awful beyond the description of my pen. During the meeting about five were converted and nine joined the church. I think this meeting has exerted a good influence in favor of Methodism. It is the first ever held by the Methodist anywhere in this section of the country. The meeting closed on Monday morning leaving some of the penitents deeply absorbed in meditation and suffused in tears."

It is doubtful that the circuit riders going from cabin to cabin and church to church could have really advanced religion in the primitive pioneer West. In fact, during the 1790s the membership in the Methodist Societies in the West actually fell off.

The campmeeting brought the scattered units of those early communities together. They faced their sins in a body and found courage to face the raw new life which they had not found before.

The Middle West of that day was tough territory. Peter Cartwright, an early campmeeting preacher stated: "Sunday was a day set apart for hunting, fishing, horse racing, card playing, balls, dances and all kinds of jollity and mirth." Dueling was common. People shot each other on the flimsiest of pretext. The frontier lured those who wanted to be free from restraint. Whisky was the common drink and the average output of the western distilleries averaged over 2 gallons per individual per year.

The noise of the campmeetings and the joys of fellowship drew people to a religious service that would never darken the door of a church. The early Methodists knew that if you drew sinners to the meetings you would have some disorders, but the good would outweigh the bad.

The campmeeting movement spread to the Urban Northeast U. S. There the campgrounds were far less rustic and even became resorts. Some displayed large ornate, enclosed tabernacles and had fancy Victorian style cottages.

The first Campmeeting in Missouri was organized in 1805 by Rev. John Clark assisted by Rev. John Walker. It was held in May and following the meeting the first class or church was organized. The next year two more classes were organized through the process of the campmeeting along Coldwater Creek. Rev. Jessie Walker assisted by Presiding Elder William McKendree reported 40 conversions at the Coldwater Campmeeting.

16 *Chapter II*

Ocean Grove Campmeeting Auditorium in 1880 which seated 5,000 people.

Bishop Asbury liked the idea of the campmeeting so much that he asked all churches to make it part of the Fourth Quarterly Conference each year. These usually began on Friday night with services held all day on Saturday and Sunday. Many of the churches had this type of meeting, but there was a second type, of longer duration, usually at a more permanent location. The Lake Creek Campmeeting was one of this latter type, drawing crowds from a larger area than the quarterly meetings and lasting at least a week.

The longer campmeetings needed to be held when the rural farmers could attend. An idea time was between planting and harvest, during August when the weather was warm and dry. This time became ideal for the preachers for that was the month before statistics were reported. New converts could be reported at the September conferences and the Methodists felt that numbers counted.

The Methodists believed that good people made a good nation and the more converts the better. The good must hurry to outnumber the bad. The campmeeting soon became a way to achieve the impossible and bring religion to the American West.

Chapter III
THE CHURCH IN THE WILDWOOD

Beginning in the 1830s and 1840s a steady stream of German immigrant settlers began to come to Pettis, Benton, and Morgan Counties in Missouri. The early settlers came up the rivers, the Missouri and the Osage, and settled on the rolling hills in the midst of the timber that reminded them of their homeland.

As early as the year 1839 some of the families felt a need for religious services. Both Methodists and Lutherans worshipped together for a while. A Methodist lay preacher by the name of Francis Walkenhorst helped organize the people together for worship. There are no official church records of this preacher but he did officiate at the weddings of Gerhardt Ringen to Adelheid Timken and John Timken and Katherine Behrens in 1840. The services were irregular and were held in homes. The fact that some organization had been done prior to the sending of the first missionary helps us understand how quickly the society at Lake Creek was organized.

The families of Cord Kahrs, Jacob Timken and Gerhard Ringen sent a petition to Dr. William Nast asking him to send a missionary to them. In the fall of 1843, Sebastian Barth was sent to organize the Osage Mission. A generally accepted method of organizing a society in those days was to hold a campmeeting and gather new converts and supporters together. We presume that the first campmeeting was held in the fall of that year and by the end of the year Barth had organized 15 preaching points. The fact that he was able to do all this lends credibility to the work of an advance preacher, Walkenhorst, coming before him. It took three weeks for Sebastian Barth to complete the 15 preaching points. He recalls his travels in this manner:

Sebastian Barth—
First Preacher assigned to Lake Creek.

> The furthest western preaching place was Lexington, the second by Brother Meyer at Freedom, near Concordia. Then 50 miles further to Brother Kahrs near Lake Creek. Eight miles to Gerhard Ringen, 15 miles to Conrad Ringen, then to Brother Gerken and Brother Timken. The next place was by Brother Schlotzhauer near Pilot Grove. Next to a German settlement 12 miles South of Boonville. Then to Boonville to preach in the English church. Then traveling through Jamestown, California, Jefferson City and finally to a point 7 miles South of Jefferson City.

17

18 Chapter III

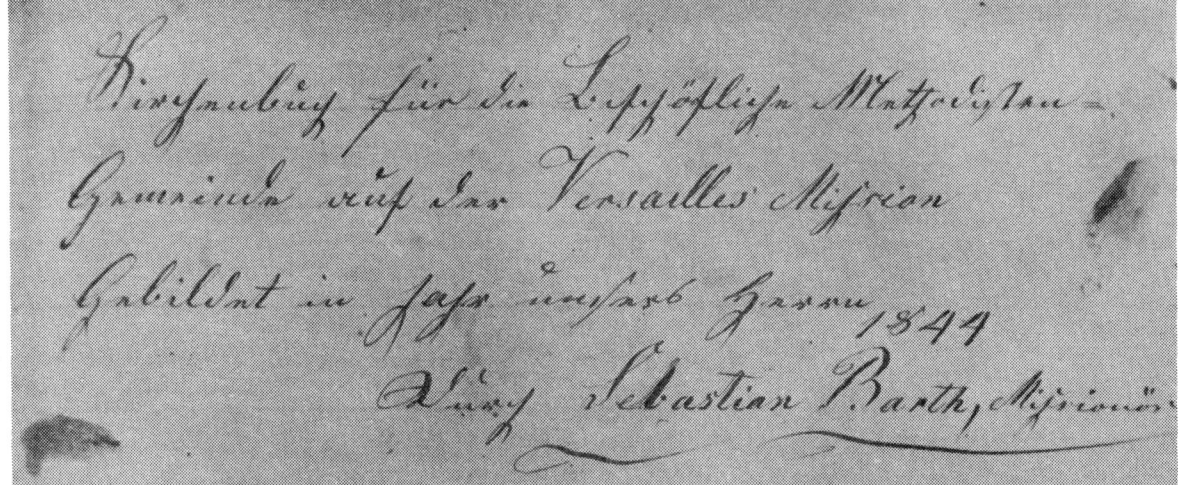

Sebastian Barth's signature in 1844 from old Lake Creek records.

The new preacher was also newly married and his wife came down with a sickness and did not want to live in what she called the "jungle house." The house in the forest at Lake Creek was on the site of the early campmeetings. Because of his wife's sickness, Barth had to travel the circuit by himself and every three weeks he would stop for a few days rest at Brother Gerkin's house at Lake Creek where he kept his books. He spent much time studying on horseback, starting his daily ride at 4AM.

In the Spring of 1844 Barth celebrated his first Whit Sunday with a service in the morning and afternoon at the forest log house. He states, "The whole house was enlightened by the presence of God and twenty souls were converted."

Campmeeting sites were normally chosen near water or creeks for the site had to provide drinking water for people and horses, dry ground, shade and timber for tentpoles and firewood. The site chosen was in section 13 of the Lake Creek Township just South of Lake Creek. A one-half acre site was purchased from Cord Miller by John Kahrs, Hermann Mahnken, Gerhardt Ringen, Louis Kahrs and Christian Rages for the purpose of building a Methodist Episcopal Church. The first church of logs was built in 1844. In 1851 this site was expanded to an acre and a half by a new indenture with Cord Miller.

Later in 1844, Barth was assigned an assistant, Heinrich Nuelson. Now they were able to add Florence, Pyrmont, Richland, and Higginsville to the rounds and still have one of them preaching at each place every two weeks instead of every three weeks. When Nuelson was sent as a helper he had to borrow $100 at 10% interest from his widowed mother, to buy a horse, saddle, and clothing. Then on a salary of $75 a year, he went off into the forest of Missouri to preach.

When the German churches were organized into districts in 1844 Dr. Ludwig Jacoby was appointed as the First Presiding Elder. He held the first Quarterly Conference of the Osage Mission at the large log home of Cord Kahrs. Those listed as present besides Dr. Jacoby were: Sebastian Barth, Henry Nuelsen, Conrad Ringen, Jacob Timken, Cord Kahrs, Henry Schlotzhauer, John Kahrs, Gerhard Ringen, Joachin Kruse, Peter Gehrken and Herman Kahrs. By the year 1845, Lake Creek had a membership of 84 and 16 preparatory members.

Barth later remembered his days on this circuit: "The work was difficult but not hopeless. Often I would ride my horse after a night service, for the large prairie flies did not bother the horses at night as they did in the day . . . the best of all is that God was with us." Barth was present at the 50th Anniversary celebration of the Mission in 1894 and stated: "The changes and enlargement is truly astonishing since 1843 when I wandered through the cow paths which stretched themselves in all directions through the prairie. Today there are beautiful cities with impressive churches, but the nicest blessing of all is that out of the small kernel of grain that was planted at that time through the preaching of God's word, hundreds of trees of justice have grown up which now stand to God's Reward and Honor."

When the split occurred in Methodism over Slavery, the Germans were strong Union supporters, but most of Missouri was of Southern Sympathy. Because of the split the German churches were assigned to the Illinois Conference in 1845. The St. Louis German District extended westward as far as Lexington and northward as far as Dubuque, Iowa and Galena, Illinois.

When Heinrich Nuelsen came to Lake Creek he was only 18 years old, yet he was given a large share of the work because of the illness of the wife of Barth. He stated the paths were to narrow to ride with a wagon so the circuit must be done on horseback. By the end of the 1844-45 year Nuelsen and Barth could report 100 new converts.

The Old Camp Grounds with the split log benches for seating.

In September of 1845, another new beginning preacher was sent to Lake Creek to replace Barth and Nuelsen. His name was Conrad Eisenmeyer. He preached at Lake Creek for two years. His helper was a local Lake Creek convert, Herman Mahnken. Herman was one of the first to join the Lake Creek Church and was licensed as an

20 Chapter III

exhorter in 1845 and served the Lake Creek Congregation for 50 years preaching whenever the appointed preacher was filling other appointments.

Rev. Eisenmeyer left Lake Creek in 1847. Let me state, that the short pastorates of that time were not due to dissatisfaction with a charge, but the Conference required the transfer of preachers at least every two years. In fact, one said. "If they can stay longer, they are probably guilty of not preaching the gospel."

The next preacher sent was William Schreck coming to serve one year from 1847-48. His first field of labor was to found the mission among the Germans at Herman Missouri. He was the first Lake Creek Preacher to have served other churches before coming to Lake Creek.

Next came Heinrich C. Dreyer for one year. He was described as energetic and a diligent worker. A photo of Rev. Dreyer is seen on this page next to the old log cabin church.

This photograph was taken in 1849 at the old log cabin, "the Cabin in the Forest" which was the home of the early circuit rider preachers. Rev. Heinrich C. Dreyer is standing at the door.

I will not list the rest of the pastor's of Lake Creek as they will be covered in detail later in this book.

The meetings at Lake Creek were probably like many other campmeetings throughout the country. Messages were long and lively and emotions were high and conversions were most important. At the campmeeting in 1849 the wife of Johann Timken walked forward to the mourners bench. Johann was not yet a Christian and tried to stop her, but Hermann Kahrs grabbed him by the throat and told him to sit and be quiet.

In 1850 the circuit was divided and the northwestern portion became the Lexington Mission and the southeastern portion continued as the Versailles Mission and sometimes listed as Florence Circuit or Lake Creek Circuit. The parsonage was always at Lake Creek.

In 1853 the church was enlarged under the ministry of Peter Hellwig. No other details about this enlargement are known.

The second Lake Creek Church building was built in 1856 on land purchased from Gerhard and Adelheid Ringen. It was about a mile northwest of the cemetery and campmeeting site and was near the old Ringen school. Thirty acres were purchased for the campmeeting grounds and church building, however, the campmeeting grounds were never moved to this location. The church and parsonage were built and served for 28 years. Trustees of the congregation at that time were: John Kahrs, Herman Mahnken, Gerhard Ringen, Louis Kahrs, Christian Rages, George Ficken, William Boecker, Herman Kahrs and Louis Momberg.

Photo at old campgrounds in 1880s.

The Campmeeting grounds were located just south of where the cemetery now sits. After the coming of the railroad in the 1860s more persons attending were living on the North side of Lake Creek and travel was sometimes difficult to campmeeting. The *Sedalia Democrat* for 1874 reports "Accidents going and coming from campmeeting . . . are getting numerous. A wagon broke down Sunday night and came in on three wheels. Last night another vehicle broke down slightly injuring a lady."

In 1878 the newspaper reports "The German Methodists are holding an old-fashioned campmeeting on the banks of the classic stream known as Lake Creek . . . . It is estimated that 1,500 persons were in attendance Sunday. A more orderly meeting was never held. They reach the sinners through their stomachs, allowing none to go away hungry."

Members still seemed to be not satisfied with the church location. Some wanted a spot of higher ground. On May 8, 1883 a business meeting was held and a prospective site a short distance Northeast of the present church was voted down. About two weeks later another meeting was held on May 23 and it was decided to buy 20 acres of land from Emma H. Jackson on which the new church should be built. This is the present location. The trustees signing the new deed were Herman

22 Chapter III

Mahnken, John Gieschen, and Peter Kahrs. The building of the new church was started immediately under the direction of Rev. John Hausam. It was officially dedicated in 1884. It was built on the highest point around and was named "Berg Zion" or Mount Zion. The old church and parsonage and the 30 acres of land were sold and the sum of $485 was realized from the sale.

Photo taken at the old campmeeting grounds near present cemetery.

For several years the campmeetings were continued at the old location near the cemetery and the original church. It is possible that the participants wanted to make sure that this is where the church would remain. Finally in the year 1891, the old cabins were torn apart, moved and rebuilt. New cabins were built on the present location, two miles north of the old grounds. Some speculate that the move was finally brought about by population patterns, but there is also a story about a typhoid scare told by some old timers.

A gently sloping area east of the church was chosen as a natural auditorium. The site for the tent tabernacle was laid out and cabins were built on the east, north and west sides of the tabernacle ground. A visiting preacher's cabin was built on the center of the south side behind the pulpit area and 100 feet southwest of it was built

The Church in the Wildwood

NORTH ↑

Cabin labels (north row, left to right): WAHLERS — RATJE/MAHRS/MEYERS — SCHLUESING — REHMER/HOEHNS — MAHRS — LEUTJEN — HINKEN

Northeast group: WIECHEN — KAHRS — HAMPY

POP STAND

GEHRS/MONSEES/HOEHNS

East column (upper): SCHROEDER — RATJE — KLEIN — PEMAND

East column (middle): NEUMEYER — RAGES/DITTMER/MONSEES — RINGEN/SIEGEL/BASS

East column (lower): HINKEN — MAHNKEN-HOEHNS-SEATON — DITZFIELD — TIPTON-HAMPY — HAMPY — RAGES

West column (upper): EICHOLZ

West column (middle-upper): GIESCHEN/BULTEMEIER — MONSEES/BLUHM — MAHNKEN/HOEHNS/CULP/WAGENKNECHT

West column (middle): BLUHM/PAGE — MAHNKEN/PAGE — PEMAND

West column (lower): LINDEMANN — KRUSE — RICHTER

TENT TABERNACLE

PREACHERS CABIN

SMITHTON PREACHERS

CABINS MARKED WITH AN ✗ ARE NO LONGER STANDING.

the Smithton Preachers Cabin. The four rows of cabins were named as streets after the first pastors of the church: Jacoby Strasse, Barth Strasse, Nuelsen Strasse and Eisenmeyer Strasse. A chart showing the known locations of cabins may be seen on the preceding page.

Campers gather during campmeeting at the old grounds next to the cemetery.

A permanent wood frame was built for the large tent tabernacle just like the one used today and three large poles supported the center. When the campgrounds were relocated and the position of the new tent decided on an event happened that we still see signs of today. At the south end of the tent the group planted 13 Oak trees. They were to represent Jesus and the 12 Disciples. The tree representing Judas was separated from the others on the southeast corner. The center tree, the Jesus tree, was planned so that one day the tent rope could be anchored on it. It stands this way today, symbolizing Jesus as the center foundation for the campmeeting.

At the turn of the century a campmeeting goer could attend up to six worship services per day. The first service usually began at 6:00AM started with the ringing of a bell. It was usually a song and prayer service. Since six to eight preachers were on hand every day there was always plenty of leadership. Before noon at least two more services were held including some Bible classes for children and young people. Following the noon meal there were two more services held in the afternoon. A break for the evening meal was held and participants were ready for the evening services. A song service usually began the evening followed by the main preaching service. Invitations were always given and many converts were witnessed.

Bernard Johansen was converted at the Lake Creek Campmeeting of 1892. He became a minister and went on to serve other German Churches. In addition to him there was Herman Mahnken, who was converted in 1844, and became a local Methodist Preacher. Others from the congregation to become ministers include:

Henry Miller, John Demand, Henry Schnakenberg, William Ratje and Wayne Hoehns. In addition four women from the congregation have become ministers' wives: Louise Demand became the wife of Rev. D. W. Smith; Katie Demand became the wife of Rev. Henry Rompel; Grace Schluesing wife of William Ratje; and Opal Monsees became the wife of Phillip Bowline.

Photo taken at old campgrounds before the year 1890.

Rev. H. H. Hackmann reported several "wonderful awakenings" while he ministered as a visiting pastor from 1891 to 1896 at Lake Creek. The power of the Lake Creek Campmeeting encouraged him and other ministers to continue their work.

One problem at the new camp grounds was that it was further from the creek. Wells were dug but they could not always be depended on in August. In a newspaper article from about 1903-5 we see more about the conditions at the Campmeeting. "The annual meeting at the Lake Creek Camp grounds which opened Friday morning closed at the night service on Tuesday. Some of those who tented on the grounds came home Tuesday night after the services, while others remained until Wednesday morning. The extreme heat and dust and the scarcity of stock water deterred some camping on the grounds, but most of the tents (cabins) were occupied and the little city in the woods throbbed with life. The crowd on Sunday was not as large as usual. A fine rain refreshed everything on Sunday about noon and another good rain came on Monday making conditions pleasant. About the same time spiritual refreshments came and penitents crowded the altars. It would be interesting to know how many have accepted Christ as their Savior and surrendered themselves to his leading in the 60 or more campmeetings that have been held on these consecrated grounds. Camping on these grounds and attending services is certainly health giving to body, mind, and soul."

The services were large in the late 1890s and early 1900s. The Crowds would sometimes number over 1,000 people. The people came from outside the Lake

26 Chapter III

Creek area, some from as far as 100 miles, however, the main support was from the nearby churches. The *Sedalia Democrat* of July 26, 1903 announced: "The Lake Creek Campmeeting Association formed by the congregations of the M. E. Churches at Smithton, Lutman, Florence and Pyrmont will have their annual meeting at the well known grounds near the Lutman Post Office beginning Thursday the 13th and closing Tuesday, the 18th of August."

A large crowd gathers around the new 1883 church building.

The biggest change that began to happen at Lake Creek was the change in language. Until 1900 all services were in German and all written records of the church were in German. The second and third generation residents were mostly bilingual and we begin to see a use of English at the campmeetings. In advertisements in the *Sedalia Democrat* for 1903 and 1904 it was stated that all services would be in German except for one English service. The *Sedalia Democrat* for Sunday, August 16, 1903 reads: "The annual German M. E. Campmeeting at Lake Creek began on Friday and will continue until next Wednesday. The exercises will be conducted in German during the meeting, except today, when a sermon will be preached in English. The next year the newspaper reported on Sunday, July 31, 1904 that: "The annual German M. E. Campmeeting at Lake Creek will be held August 5-10, inclusive, says the *Smithton Sunbeam*. The meeting will be conducted by J. H. Asling, Ph.D. assisted by the following ministers: Revs. True of Cincinnati, treasurer of the Deacons' home; Professors Kriege and Wipperman of Warrenton; D. W. Smith and E. Asling of Kansas City; Woestermeyer of Concordia; Buechner of Sedalia; Rademacher of Smithton; Ahrens of Pyrmont; Crepin of Lake Creek; and others.

In the *Smithton Sunbeam* the 1907 campmeeting was announced as: "The German Methodist Episcopal Camp-meeting will be held at the campground August 8 to 13th. There will be a number of prominent ministers from a distance among whom are Reverends J. H. Asling, O. E. Kriege, D. E. Smith, W. T. Islez, C. G. Meyer and Otto Gnefin. There will be an English sermon on Sunday afternoon by a prominent minister. All are cordially invited to attend."

The ring of Fellowship around the tabernacle at Lake Creek in the early 1900s.

Another article appeared in the *Sedalia Democrat*: "The Lake Creek German campmeeting will open Friday the 19th of August (1910) at 2 O'clock in the afternoon. Professor Kriege of Warrenton; Rev. A. Jungmeyer of Kansas City, Kansas; Rev. H. Ahrens of Endor, Kansas; and Rev. R. D. Winken of Concordia will officiate. District Superintendent D. W. Smith will be absent until Sunday as he will be attending a meeting in Higginsville. These along with Revs. Meyer of Lake Creek, Tanner of Smithton, Hermann of Sedalia and Woestermeyer of Stover are the ministers expected to be present. There are between 40 and 50 frame houses on the grounds. An average of about three families will occupy each cabin, and the little city with its shady streets will be vocal with song and praise from Friday until Wednesday."

With the advent of the World War, the use of German became very unpopular and all services at Lake Creek were conducted in English.

In an undated report from sometime around 1910 we see this insight: "Reports from the Lake Creek German Campmeeting say that while the attendance of those who own tents is good, some are unable to attend on account of scarcity of water and pastures at home. The attendance was good on Sunday. There was an address in English on Education by Rev. Tuschoff, of Warrenton college and an English sermon by Rev. Housen (probably Hausam). Rev. Zwingli Meyer, pastor at Urich, preached a sermon in English on Monday. The preachers in attendance were: District Superintendent D. W. Smith; Rev. Tuschoff of Warrenton college; Rev. Jacob Tanner of Smithton; Rev. Hermann of Sedalia; Rev. Kalkenbach (Kaltenbach) of Kansas City; Rev. Northdurft of Pyrmont; and Florence and Rev. G. F. Meyers of

Lake Creek. The campers returned to their homes on Wednesday. There were a large number of conversions."

Lake Creek Church at the turn of the Century before the bell tower and German Room were added.

The Pyrmont Church was also known as the Hinken Church and was active in the campmeeting until it closed in 1921. They combined with the German Methodist Episcopal Church in Stover.

Other changes came about over the years. Lighting for the evening services was simply camp fires at first, then fire stands were built on mounds of earth at the corners of the tent. Later Oil Lamps were hung from brackets mounted on the trees. Later acetylene lamps were used which were replaced by a Delco Battery system and finally in 1949 real electricity arrived as the Rural Electric Cooperative put in power lines.

Refrigeration was also a problem. A hole was dug for ice and was filled with sawdust as insulation. Ice was cut from the ponds or creek in the winter and was stored under sawdust until the summer meeting time. Because of the lack of refrigeration, only certain items could be brought to the meeting site. A pie would have to be used the first day since they would spoil quickly. Bread was rolled in cloth and stored in cupboards in the cabins. Bacon or other meat was often fried down before coming and recooked in its own grease for a meal. Shortly after the turn of the century many cabins had their own ice box; but only in recent years, with the addition of heavier wiring for electricity, have refrigerators been used.

Front row: Henry E. Hoehns with Leo, Henry Ringen, Anna Ringen, Mary Ratje-Hoehns, J. H. Hoehns and Rev. G. J. Jaiser;
Back row: August Hoehns, Laura Hoehns, August Dittmer, Laura Dittmer, Elizabeth Hoehns-Mahnken, Emelia Hampy, Julia Rages-Hoehns, Mary Bluhm-Rages, Elsie Hoehns and Arni Siegel.

According to the article included in the 1906 Souvenir of the West Deutschen Konferenz, the Lake Creek Campmeeting had about 40 cabins with 50 to 75 families staying each night during the meetings.

The coming of the automobile also brought changes to Lake Creek. There were very few cars at first since they were expensive, not always dependable and sometimes unable to pass through the dirt roads of the area. In 1914 only three families owned a car in the Lake Creek area. Before the coming of the automobile the men would often ride a horse back to the home and do chores during the day and return to be with the family at night. The advent of cars meant that people could come and go more often from the campmeeting. Once a family got a car they might only come for an evening meeting and not for the entire day.

This began to change the attendance habits of participants and gradually the number of worship services offered each day changed. At the turn of the century up to six services per day were held. By the 1940s five services were held each day and by the 1950s it was down to four per day. Today the evening service is the only daily service with Bible Classes held every weekday morning.

In 1919, after several meetings and much discussion, an addition was made to the building. The entire building was jacked up and with pick and shovel a basement was dug and concrete poured. Also at this time the "German Room" and the bell tower and vestibule were added. The dirt and rocks removed from the basement area were hauled by wagons and teams to the north end of the camp ground where in the woods you can still see a ridge of dirt and rocks today. It was hard work with no motorized assistance.

30 Chapter III

Western row of cabins in 1950s.

Stained Glass windows were also purchased and brought from St. Louis. This large project was done during the ministry of Rev. Oscar F. Kettlekamp and involved a lot of effort on his part.

On November 16, 1919 an all day program was planned for the dedication of the building. A basket dinner for the noon hour and the Presiding Elder, Dr. H. A. Hohenwald was to preach the dedicatory sermon. The congregation was unaware of the Methodist rules that stated a building could have a ground breaking or a consecration ceremony before being paid for, but no dedication service could be held until all bills were paid and the building was free from debt. This announcement by the Presiding Elder came as quite a shock to the Lake Creek people. The debt was about $2,500.00 but the people pooled their resources together and raised that amount on the spot and the dedication was held as planned.

The last major remodeling project on the church was completed in 1971 when the basement was enlarged and the kitchen and bathroom areas added. This gave much needed space for the many fine dinners cooked at Lake Creek.

In 1973 the sanctuary was carpeted and soon afterwards a new electronic organ was installed. In 1975 and 1976 the windows were covered with plexiglas or storm windows.

The parsonage was remodeled and new cabinets built in the kitchen in 1989. In 1990 new vinyl siding was installed on the church.

The *Sedalia Democrat* of August 16, 1936 reports: "A number of Tipton people are attending the Lake Creek Campmeeting during its convenings. Mrs. S. R. Ferguson of the Tipton Methodist Church is director of Music for the meeting and Rev. C. C. Vanzant was in charge of Saturday evening.

In August of 1938 the following report was written. "The 93rd Campmeeting closed on Sunday night after an eight day session. More than a dozen ministers were present during the campmeeting and had part in the program. Rev. Rompel of Ottawa, Illinois preached each evening. He has traveled extensively and was a most interesting and inspirational speaker. Plans were made for ground and camp improvement and the committee report is given below. The present site for the camp grounds was established 47 years ago (1891) having been moved from a place south of the present site. The posts and supports for the tent were erected then and many of them are in bad condition and will not support the tent another year."

The Lake Creek congregation gathered with Bishop Ivan Lee Holt in the summer of 1952.

"It is hoped that a more permanent tabernacle may be erected in the near future and it was decided to erect the frame work before another year. The past year it was necessary to dig a well for use during the campmeetings. The old well used for many years caved in following last years campmeeting. Funds to take care of all current expenses and to pay for the drilling of the well were provided for during the session."

Report of Special Committee on recommendations for Lake Creek Campmeeting, August 12, 1938.

> We rejoice in the 93 years of the Lake Creek Campmeeting. These have been years rich in Christian Fellowship and spiritual influences. Our Fathers built better than they knew and these many years attest to their faith and love of God. Times have changed, but the Gospel Truths still remain and today we rejoice in the rich blessings we are enjoying at this camp.
>
> We anticipate the 100th Anniversary of the founding of the Lake Creek Campmeeting. Time brings decay and change and to meet the needs of these modern times, we must improve the properties and continue to enlarge. The committee desires therefore to make some recommendations which we believe will add much to the material comforts of all and assure the perpetuity of the campmeeting.

1. We want to most heartily record our approval of the action of cottage owners and board members in their meeting on Friday in their recommendation of the improvement of the tabernacle with a new and substantial framework and other improvements.
2. We suggest some needed repairs of the seats and the construction of some new seats.
3. Each cabin owner is urged to repair and make more attractive and livable the cottages.
4. The care of the trees and the planting of young shade trees to take the place of those which have been removed is urged for this fall and next spring.
5. We solicit our friends to erect new and attractive cottages and to secure a larger number of campers during the time of the annual campmeeting.
6. We suggest a larger advertisement of the annual meeting and greater effort to increase attendance.
7. We recommend the appointment of a committee on cottages and grounds to secure better care of the properties and the encouragement of people to erect new cottages. To assist in their work, we suggest that the cottage owners and friends as far as possible contribute 50 cents or more per annum as a clean up fund.
8. We request each cottage provide an enclosed garbage can and that arrangements be made to gather daily the garbage, thus adding to the sanitation.
9. We recommend that the program committee have an early meeting and make advanced plans for the annual meeting.
10. We pledge our financial support that all obligations may be met and improvements made and properly financed.
11. We most earnestly solicit the sympathy and good will of the people of this entire section of the state and your help that this old campmeeting may continue more largely to contribute to the social and religious life of the people.
12. We pledge anew our support to the officers and workers of the association and to each other for greater interest and devotion to this campmeeting that is laboring together and with God we may see the coming day more glorious than in the past. In unity there is strength and an enthusiastic devotion will bring the desires of our hearts. This is God's work, may we so labor that He may crown it with success.

Signed by the committee,
Frank Monsees
August Klein
August Dittner
Leo Hoehns
Charles Bohling
Elmer Culbertson
E. I. LaRue

Photo taken in 1952.

The recommended new tabernacle was never built but there was interest in continuing improvements. This led to a new constitution of the Campmeeting Association in 1941. The entire text of this document in included in the appendix in the back of this book.

Reading left to right, front row: Bishop Ivan Lee Holt, Linda Pauline Demand, Rev. J. C. Paschal—Pastor, Glenda Aurelia Teter, Dr. E. W. Bartley—D. S.;
Second row: Gary Allen Eichholz, Charles Edward Bybee, Agnes Anderson, Virgil Schlobohm;
Back row: Kenneth Dale Monsees, Claude Eugene Page, Charles L. Bultemeier, Ralph Dale Montgomery.

The *Sedalia Democrat* of Sunday, August 4, 1940 reports: "The Lake Creek Campmeeting will be held at the Lake Creek Methodist Church, eight miles south of Smithton, August 10 to 18, it was announced by Rev. L. M. Starkey, District Superintendent of the Sedalia District of the Methodist Church. Rev. E. T. Raney of

Marshall will give the Bible Lectures each week day at 9:30A.M. and Dr. Paul Durham, pastor of the Union Avenue Methodist Church in St. Louis will preach twice each day at 2:30P.M. and 8:00 P. M. The first services, Dr. Durham preaching, will be held Saturday evening August 10th at 8:00P.M. Sunday, August 11th has been designated Sedalia Day for Methodist Churches, except during the time of regular services in Sedalia. Rev. E. L. Rathert is pastor at Lake Creek.

A few old flyers still exist that give some insight as to the happenings of the Lake Creek Campmeeting in recent years. In 1946 the daily schedule started at 6:30AM with a Morning Watch held by Rev. H. S. Anglin, District Superintendent. Preaching services were held at 10:30AM, 2:15PM, 3:30PM and the Evening service started at 8:15PM following a song service. In the afternoon Rev. Ralph Hurd led the youth at 2:30PM and Vacation Bible School was held with Mrs. W. J. Holtzen as leader assisted by Martha Monsees and Evelyn Page. Other preachers involved that year were: Rev. E. L. Thomas, Rev. Arthur S. Olsen, and Rev. E. F. Dillon. Mrs. Stanley Ferguson of Tipton was the Song Leader.

Ruth Evelyn Green and Bernice Hoehns were listed as pianists. Rev. E. L. Rathert was the Lake Creek Pastor. Due to shortages still existing from war time the meals were to be in sandwich form served by the ladies of the church. All were invited to camp free, bringing tents and/or bedding.

The theme of campmeeting for 1950 was "Christ Came To Save Sinners." The leaders were Rev. E. W. Bartley, District Superintendent of Sedalia District; Rev. Ralph Hurd and Rev. H. U. Campbell of Sedalia; Rev. E. F. Dillon of Smithton; and Rev. S. A. Gardner of Lincoln, Mo. Mrs. Ava Pitchford of Sweet Springs was the youth leader, Mrs. Stanley Rages and Mrs. Marie Brauer were in charge of Children's hour. Theresa Cook and Dorothy Ann Bass played the piano. Rev. H. B. Fly was the Lake Creek Pastor.

In 1952 Campmeeting was held from August 3-10 with Rev. A. G. Pontious, Rev. John Moberly, and Rev. Wendell Grout as speakers. The VanKoevering Family from Coopersville, Michigan were the Musical Evangelists. Rev. J. Ralph Sipes of Holden was in charge of feeding the multitude offering "good food at reasonable prices." The schedule for the week days in 1952 was as follows:

Awakening Bell	6:00AM
Call to Prayer	6:30AM
Breakfast Hour	7:00AM
Minister's Retreat	8:00AM
First General Service and Young Peoples Hour	10:30AM
Dinner Hour	NOON
Second General Service and Children's Hour	2:30PM
Third General Service	4:00PM
Supper	5:30PM
Experience Meeting	7:30PM
Song and Musical Festival	8:00PM
All Out Evangelistic Preaching	8:30PM
Starlight Praise Service	9:45PM

The Days were full and active for all.

Following the appointment of Rev. J. C. Paschal in September of 1952 he began a camp ground improvement. Members were urged to donate either one gallon of paint or one hours labor and all the cabins that were fit to repair would be painted. He suggested they be painted in a choice of six colors: White, Orange, Green, Brown, Red, and Blue. The following poem was printed in the promotion:

> He's on his way to campmeeting;
> Knowing there awaits fond greeting;
> From old time friends, long time not seen,
> He expectantly climbs the last hill,
> He stops, listens, looks. O what a thrill.
> *Camp's* all painted White, Brown, Blue, Green.
> Hallelujah! It's like a dream!!!

This did lead to some improvements on some of the cabins but the paint project never received popular support and so the cabins continued their rustic look. In 1952 under the pastorate of Rev. J. Coleson Paschal the church began printing fine magazine format newsletter. The photos and articles contained in this effort are very interesting. In 1953 area towns were each assigned a day. Sunday began the week with Sedalia day, followed by Smithton Day, Stover-Florence Day, Tipton Day, Windsor Day, Cole Camp Day on Saturday, and finally ending with Sunday, The Lord's Day for all. Speakers that year were Prince Benjamin Dennis from Africa, Rev. Harold Jesnen, Rev. Paul C. Paschal, and Rev. Llewellyn Younge, an American Indian as Music Director. Leola Paschal and Ralph Hurd were the Youth Directors and the W. S. C. S. in charge of the children's hour. Dorothy Ann Culp and Mary Theresa Cook were pianists. That year there were no morning or afternoon services on Monday, Tuesday or Wednesday of the week.

Joshua Tein, evangelist is seen in the right center of this picture of the people under the tent in 1955.

Today the Lake Creek Tent Tabernacle is still erected as in the past, the tent is laid out, center poles are positioned, and then the tent itself is raised by block and tackle.

After the tent fabric is raised on the center poles the tent is secured to the frame by ropes. Phillip Monsees and George Cook are seen here.

The Church in the Wildwood 37

By the next year the morning services were phased out but a 2:00PM preaching service was held every afternoon. Rev. Jeff Marsh was the evangelist for the week. Other leaders listed were Rev. Robert Lehew, Rev. Toby Tucker, Rev. Harry Smith, Rev. Noel Clark Holt, Rev. H. E. Marshall, Rev. J. H. DeVries, Rev. Lee Soxman, Rev. Ralph Hurd, Rev. E. L. Hobbs, Rev. Russell Estes, and Rev. William Butts. Pianists were listed as Darlene Meyer, Mrs. Lawrence Grupe, Dorothy Ann Culp and Lois Hoehns with Mrs. Russell Estes in charge of music.

The old benches are removed from storage in the cabins and cleaned in preparation. Bertha Cook and Kathy Page are seen here.

Tabernacle in the 1960s.

38 Chapter III

The year 1955 saw the Monday, Tuesday and Wednesday times have only the 8PM evening preaching service. The main speaker that year was the Rev. Joshua Tien, conference evangelist

In 1959, Bishop Ivan Lee Holt was the guest speaker at the afternoon and evening services. Services were again held every afternoon that year and for the first time in six years morning services were held Wednesday through Saturday. The ladies of the church served lunch and supper during the meeting.

During the 1960's the morning services were again discontinued and the afternoon services were held only Wednesday through Saturday. The evening services continued to be the big event. In 1964, Dr. W. B. Selah, vice president of Central Methodist College was the featured speaker. In 1967, Dr. Kenneth Johnson was the featured evening speaker.

The Tent Tabernacle in the 1970s looking from the southwest.

In 1971, Rev. Roy Sribling from Gashland United Methodist Church in Kansas City spoke each evening on the theme "Christ makes the Difference." Rev. Allen Pruitt of Knobnoster was placed in charge of young adult activities to be held at 9:15PM each evening. The afternoon children's time had now become a Vacation Church School under the direction of Darlene Meyer. Jerry Moon was the Host Pastor and Debra Cook was pianist.

In 1972 a different event was linked to the campmeeting. The first four evenings were preaching services featuring Dr. Sterling Ward, District Superintendent from Springfield who had grown up in Stover and attended campmeetings as a child. Other speakers were Rev. Charles Burner and Rev. Ed Neimeyer. The last four days of campmeeting were as part of a Lay Witness Mission with team members from 15 churches participating.

In 1974 the Campmeeting Board had a new building constructed housing two modern restrooms and four shower stalls. This was a great help to those who stayed nights during the week. The old four and five seater outhouses were no longer used, however, remnants of them may still be seen in the woods. Also that year several areas were cleared for recreational vehicles to park and camp. By 1974 only the evening service was held on weekdays and Vacation Church School was held every weekday morning. The featured speakers that week were "Tank" Harrison formerly of the Memphis Police Department and Hugh Smith, a former Air Force Pilot.

In 1979 a severe storm destroyed the tent and a fund was immediately raised to purchase a new tent, the one still in use today. Bookmarks were made from the old tent fabric and were used as keepsakes by the participants. In 1979 the two featured speakers were Rev. George Burgin and Rev. Hubert Neth. Song Leaders were Rachael Gieschen and Dan Adkison. A watermelon feed for all was scheduled for the final Sunday afternoon. Prior to that year the melons had been furnished by Rev. & Mrs. Phillip Bowline who were then living in the Lake Creek Parsonage.

In 1981 only evening services were held in addition to the regular Sunday Morning worship. Rev. Paul Metcalf was the speaker for the entire week. In 1982 Rev. J. D. Little was the week long evangelist and Rev. Fred Royer was the song leader. In 1983 Rev. James Bryan was the evening speaker and Rev. Ed. Neimeyer and Rev. Marie Hyatt preached the Sunday Morning services.

The year of 1984 began the practice of a variety of speakers during campmeeting. That year speakers were: Rev. Paul Metcalf, Rev. James Bryan, Rev. J. D. Little, Rev. Paul White, Rev. George Burgin, Rev. Hubert Neth, Rev. Lee Whiteside, Rev. Ralph LaForge and Rev. Charles Caldwell. That was the year that Rev. Caldwell came to campmeeting on horseback dressed as John Wesley.

In 1986 the practice of Dinner on the Grounds was reestablished and the Bible School during weekday mornings recreated a village as it might have been in the time of Jesus. Electric outlets were also made for three Recreational vehicle sites allowing more comfort for some campers. The speakers that year were: Rev. Harry Foockle, Rev. Elroy Hines, Rev. Manning Miller, Rev. Prentice Wilbanks and Rev. Hubert Neth. In that year Rev. Seaton, Lake Creek Pastor, began organizing afternoon activities for the youth. In 1987 the speakers were: Rev. Steve Johnson, Rev. Frank Marlin, Rev. Harry Foockle, and Rev. Hubert Neth.

The year 1988 saw the following speakers: Rev. Joe Comer, Rev. Ron Page, Rev. Phil Neimeyer and Rev. Steve Cox.

In 1989 four preachers were listed as speakers: Rev. Ed. Neimeyer, Wendy Whiteside, Rev. Champ Breeden and Rev. Randy Gilmore. The same pattern held true for 1990 with Rev. Jim Bryan, Rev. Harry Foockle, Rev. Asher McDaniel and Rev. Hubert Neth. This pattern of four or more speakers will probably continue as it is increasingly impossible to arrange for a Pastor to be away from his/her church for more than a few days.

In 1992 a new shelter house building was constructed and will greatly improve the facilities at the grounds.

The Lake Creek Youth were organized in 1892 as "The Jugenbund." In the years of German unpopularity just before the First World War the name of the Youth Group was changed to the "Epworth League" in order to conform to the other English speaking Methodist Churches. The Epworth League through a number of projects sponsored a stained glass window on the north in the German Room in the new addition of 1919. In 1940 after unification the name was changed to the Methodist Youth Fellowship and in 1969 the name changed to the United Methodist

Youth Fellowship. The current youth group not only serves the youth of the Lake Creek church, but also youth from surrounding area churches.

The women of Lake Creek were organized as "The Women's Foreign Missionary Society" in 1887 by Miss Margarethe Dreyer, a deaconess from Chicago, Illinois, and sister of the current Lake Creek Pastor, J. H. Dreyer. No records of this organization exist today and nothing is known as to the number of years it was in existence.

In October of 1922 the ladies were reorganized as a group known as the "Helping Hands." Mrs. A. B. Schowengerdt, wife of the pastor was the first president and Mrs. John Schluesing was the second president who served. There were 37 charter members of the "Helping Hands." The Society's theme song was: "There is much we can do if we work with a will." In 1926 when the German churches were united with the English speaking congregations the group became known as the "Ladies Aid."

In 1940 with the union of the three branches of Methodism the name was again changed to the "Woman's Society of Christian Service," or WSCS. In 1972 they reorganized and became the present "United Methodist Women." They also celebrated their 50th Anniversary at that time.

Davidson Methodist Campground near Arkadelphia, Arkansas dates back to 1884.

Although many of the old campmeeting sites are now vacant and not even remembered by the neighborhood, the Lake Creek campmeeting continues on. Many of the campmeetings that do continue today now have plush tabernacles, ceiling fans, etc. One in Texas has even glassed in its tabernacle and has air conditioning. Some such as Davidson Campground in Arkansas are large in numbers of cabins occupied (200 plus), but the attendance at worship is not much different than Lake Creek. As one camper there put it: "It used to be that people were more religious and less civilized. Today they are more civilized and less religious. The cabins are used more for a vacation and recreation rather than the worship and renewal being the center of the event.

To see the Lake Creek Campmeeting today brings the visitor a feeling of having somehow stepped backward in time. Most of the cabins are at least 100 years old and all lack such modern items as paint, glazing, screening and plumbing. The large tent tabernacle stands in the center. Although today there are modern restrooms and showers, a new shelter house for dinners and activities, as well as places for modern RV's to hookup; these are on the perimeter and do not detract from the feeling. The campgrounds have come to life every August since 1843 and gospel preaching still is heard today. There were two years when service could not be held. In 1863 when campers gathered but services could not be held due to snipers; and in 1901 when a severe drought stopped the session. The lack of these two sessions as official full meetings accounts for the discrepancy stated in 1930's and 40's flyers, in which 1938 was listed as the 93rd, not the 95th session, although it was the 95th year.

The tent at Lake Creek as it appears today.

Many of the participants at today's Lake Creek Campmeetings will tell you they met their spouse at campmeeting. These marriages have something to do with the complex kinship networks that exist today among cabin owners. While it is a temptation to say people like to come together because they are kin, the reverse is also true. People are kin because they have camped together over these many years.

Although the Lake Creek Campmeeting has always been officially Methodist it is today and always has been non-denominational in character. In the campmeeting today a real sense of community can still be found. It is a refuge from a world of alienation where every one is friendly and knows the others are also "good people." Children can play together and families who share the same values can relax together. It is this changeless feel of the Lake Creek Campmeeting that is important. A stable environment where one can still center their thoughts on their relationship with God. The old time religion is still preached in the tent, even though some may lament its coolness compared to days past.

Chapter III

The history of the Lake Creek Campmeeting is not so much a history of dates, facts, and statistics, as it is a history of spiritual experiences. It is more than just a location, it is a fellowship . . . it is a place to be spiritually fed.

Chapter IV
THE CLOUD OF WITNESSES

Rev. Henry Edward Rompel was the minister at Lake Creek in 1900 to 1901 and in 1943 sent his regrets to the 100th anniversary gathering with the words: "Give my greetings and blessings to all, may you have a real spiritual up-lift as you think of the cloud of witnesses still here and the many who have gone. Someday we too shall be with them as the people of God. They shall come from the North and South, from the East and West, to sit down in the Kingdom of God together. That will be a real campmeeting time. Glory to God."

The following are taken from interviews from members of that "Cloud of Witnesses" and give us further insights into the Lake Creek Campmeeting.

Families gather at the old campgrounds in 1880s.

Lillie Siegel first attended camp meting at Lake Creek with her grandmother when she was 11 or 12 years old. She attended regularly for the next 80 years until the late 1980's. Her earliest memory is the fun they had sleeping in the big straw bed that stretched across the cabin. She remembered many more services than today. The morning began with a prayer service with many still in their night caps. There were always one or two services before lunch and then again in the afternoon and finally the day was capped off with the evening service. She remembered singing German hymns. Many of the young people could read and sing the German hymns but didn't understand the meaning of the words they were singing.

43

Bluhm and Rages families at site of old Campmeeting grounds (present-day Lake Creek Cemetery) prior to 1890.

Back Row: Dietrich Bluhm, Charles Rages, Tom Bluhm, Katharine Gehrs-Bluhm, John Bluhm behind Albert Rages, Ellen Rages-Siegel behind Albert Neumeyer, Fritz Siegel holding son John W., Julia Rages, Christian G. Rages, Anna Rages, Julia LaFrenz-Neumeyer, Maria LaFrenz-Schluesing and Martin Neumeyer;

Middle Row: Katharina Kastens-Bluhm holding Bessie, Heinrich Bluhm, Adelheid Röhrs-Bluhm, Mary Bluhm-Rages holding Wesley F., John Rages holding Laura M., Louis Bluhm holding Henry, Wilhelmina Munsterman-Bluhm holding John F.;

Front Row: Dennis Bluhm, Tina Bluhm, Leota Bluhm, Emelia Rages, Curtis Bluhm, Ella Bluhm, Lillie Bluhm, Clara Bluhm and Ed Rages.

Laura Kruse was three years old when she attended her first campmeeting at Lake Creek. She remembered that when she was young there was great anticipation in all the children as families prepared to go to campmeeting. The girls always had new dresses so that they would look nice and they would need them for school soon anyway. Getting the food ready was fun. For several days there was bread baking and coffee cake making and finally pies. They also had several kinds of jams and jellies they had made. These were all packed in a large solid oak chest that her parents had brought from Germany. The bread was put on shelves on one end and cakes and pies on the other end. The baked goods had to last all week. When they arrived at their cabin they would divide it by hanging curtains into a bedroom and a living/dining room. A kitchen was built on the back where they cooked on a wood stove. Her father went back and forth every day to take care of the chores. He would often bring back fresh milk and roasting ears. They kept their butter fresh by keeping it wrapped in a damp cloth and if you kept it damp the evaporation cooled it. That was the only way of refrigeration. Laura attended campmeeting at both the old camp grounds by the cemetery and at the present location.

Harry Monsees was born in 1874 when the campmeeting was only 30 years old. In 1976 at the age of 102 he was interviewed by Rev. Phillip Bowline. He recalled his family going to campmeeting and staying several days. Their camp place was next to the cemetery. The older boys in the family had to go home each day and do chores. There was a spring or well about halfway down the hill toward the creek and the campers all got their water there. It became contaminated and typhoid fever broke out. His brother Rudy was one of those afflicted. After the spring was contaminated they would go down to Lake Creek with barrels and bring water to the camp grounds. When asked if the tainted water was the reason for the camp grounds being moved in 1891 he said "No, they just wanted a better and higher place." They also would not have to cross the creek as much.

Left to right: Sophia Siegel, Mary Rages, Margaretha Hoehns, and Anna Harper.

Ruth Bultemeier has been attending campmeeting all her life. She loved the long row of huge maple trees that were along the east side of the cabins and remembers one day when a rattlesnake in one of the trees caused quite a bit of excitement. She remembers more cabins. Some have been torn down and others destroyed by fire. The tent tabernacle is much the same today but it used to be much taller. She remembers the preaching being more on fire with more insistence on coming to the mourners bench. The older men would sit in the front corners, known as the Amen Corners and shout Amen to what the preacher said. When the call came at the end of the service, everyone was pretty worked up and ready to go forward. At first she remembers everyone bringing their own food from home, but when the ladies started serving meals it became three meals a day at 25 cents per

46 *Chapter IV*

meal. After a few years they began to see there were people coming to eat and not staying for campmeeting so they cut back on serving meals and began to take more meals in the cabins. Ruth remembers her grandfather loading up the bell that was used to start the meetings. He brought it every year and the same bell was used until a few years ago. The evening services always ended with an altar call and the week always ended with a double circle with everyone shaking hands with everyone else and singing "God Be With You Till We Meet Again."

Elmer Bultemeier came to campmeeting all his life even though his family didn't belong to Lake Creek they would come by wagon from Florence. Since they didn't have a cabin they ate out under the trees. He remembered when most of the boards on the cabins were still solid and in good shape and the tent was white and much taller. The preachers were loud and strong. Since his family lived away they usually came only for Sunday and stayed for three services.

Fred Ditzfeld's Sunday School Class.
Front: Dr. William Reynolds, Vernon Demand, Fred Ditzfeld, Roy Demand, Ed Rages;
Back: Louis Kahrs, Ben Mahnken, Ben Rehmer, Fred Dittmer, —?—, Milo Culbertson.

Hattie Gieschen remembered that she attended campmeeting all her life except for one year when she was sick. The Monday before campmeeting was always wash day, getting all the pretty new clothes starched and pressed. Tuesday was spent baking bread and cakes and packing up the clothes and bedding. Early on Wednesday they would load up the wagon and head for the camp ground. The men would work to put up the large tent and the meeting would usually begin with a service that evening. One of her earliest memories was getting dressed up for services. All the singing and preaching was in German before World War I. She didn't learn to speak English until she started school. Her parents always spoke German to each other but some times they used some English at home. She remembers gas lanterns and later acetylene lights being used until electricity was installed.

Ed Schlobohm knew he was attending campmeeting at least by 1917. He remembers standing room only at some of the meetings. His wife, Buelah first came to the meetings with him. Before electricity he hauled Ice for the concession stand. It was brought in 100 pound blocks and covered with sawdust to keep it frozen. Sometimes on Sunday night they would bring in 10 gallons of Ice Cream and sell it for five cents a cone. He remembered one year they weren't allowed to have the concession stand on the grounds so they had it across the road.

Leo Hoehns attended over 80 campmeeetings since his parents brought him as a baby. He remembered bigger crowds and more interesting meetings. There was more fire-and-brimstone preaching and folks were more bent on saving souls. Leo furnished the bell that today rings at the start of each session. Leo stated "It's great to see the youth involved. Many have gone on from here to success. Jacob Timken invented the roller bearing and is buried in the Lake Creek Cemetery and a manufacturing company today bears his name."

Wesley Rages remembered that in 1957 they had to get a new canvas tent. The old one was then 52 years old and had been patched several times.

The Campgrounds in 1952.

Claude Page has been coming to campmeetings for over 70 years. His parents joined the Lake Creek congregation in 1922 when he was two years old and they brought Claude and eight siblings to the gathering. They were not related to the German families in the area. He remembers: "We would stay all week . . . we didn't own a cabin but we always managed to either use Henry Ringen's cabin and in later years the Wiechen cabin . . . . They wasn't usin(sic) them and they'd let us stay in them. There was always time for games between services. The men could be found playing horseshoes while children played Annie-over the Tabernacle with green persimmons. Sometimes the boys would sneak away from the hot afternoon services and go swimming in Lake Creek. He remembers that after his family got a car they didn't stay as many nights. A trip to the refreshment stand was a welcome diversion for the youth. Claude remembers a local man putting up a refreshment stand across the road about 1933. "There was a time when . . . you weren't allowed to smoke on the camp grounds . . . Old Jim Bridges put up a stand over to the north across the road."

48 *Chapter IV*

Evelyn Wagenknecht Page, Claude's wife, remembers that she stayed on the opposite side of the campground from Claude's family because she was from Smithton and the Smithton cabins were on the west side of the campground. In 1948-50 they bought one of the cabins for the big sum of $15. Evelyn lived in Smithton with her aunt and uncle. She often went to campmeeting with her best friend, Nadine Demand Moore.

Nadine Demand Moore had grandparents who were members of the German Church at Smithton and kept a cabin at Lake Creek. She remembers her grandmother and other older adults speaking in German. We would sit lots of times . . . and they would try to teach us German Songs. The children were rarely successful at learning more than a few words of the language. After the war most youngsters showed little interest in learning the language of their grandparents.

Confirmation Class at John Schluesing's Home.
Front: Grace Schluesing-Ratje, Opal Monsees-Bowline, Rev. Walter C. Wagner, Viola Rages, Hulda Wiechen-Anderson;

Back: Edgar Wiechen, Hulda Ditzfeld-Monsees, Minter Ringen, Elsie Hoehns-Culp, Logan Siegel.

Elsie Culp attended campmeeting for over 80 years and remembered that the preachers have changed from hell preaching-pulpit pounding and spit flying speakers to a much calmer breed today. Elsie was just a teenager in the 1910's and remembered that the crowds were much larger and sometimes over flowed the tent and sometimes had to sit on the ground around the area because there were no benches. The pop and candy stand has been around a long time. The pop was kept iced down in wash tubs. The Bowlines and Monsees had a watermelon feed that has now become a part of the camp association activities. The preacher's cabin was in the center directly to the south of the tent. The visiting preachers stayed there overnight. They ate their meals with different families, with most of the families taking a turn. During the 1940s the women offered meals served at the church. The Sunday meal would always be the biggest.

Marriage of Harry W. Hampy and Emelia A. Rages, April 8, 1909, performed by Rev. Gottlob J. Jaiser.

Melford Monsees states that he has been coming to campmeeting all his life and that is, since babies have worn long dresses. His first real memory is going to campmeeting with his grandfather with a wagon full of provisions. He said it seemed to be a long, long way from Smithton to Lake Creek. He was probably about five years old that year and although he was having a good time he still began to get homesick. He remembers going home with an uncle in mid-week. Later when he came with his mother and sister he enjoyed the good times with the young people. A favorite game was throwing balls or green persimmons over the tent tabernacle. Other favorites were going through the woods and having pop and ice cream at the stand. The cabins were built so that the men could sleep in a loft and the women and girls slept below. The women could not climb the ladders in their dresses. One could wake up to the smell of breakfast cooking in the morning and listening to the women laugh and talk as they began their day. The preaching was more evangelistic many years ago and he remembers some of the preachers shouting and pounding the pulpit. There were many more conversions in those days with many youth coming to the altar area. There was a period of decline in attendance but he is encouraged that it is beginning to pick up in recent years. The number of people staying over is much less. Almost every cabin and space was once full of campers.

50 Chapter IV

He believes that every Bishop of the Methodist Church of Missouri has preached at campmeeting.

Opal Bowline stated that her family would usually go out on Friday and stay until Tuesday . . . (Father would) have to go back and forth at least once a day and if we had cows that we were milking at that time then he'd have to go home in the morning and then again at night. He usually stayed all night. Opal believes that campmeeting was affected by cars. Cars allowed travel back and forth more often and people did not have to stay as long at the meetings. She remembers attending Bible School in Smithton and she learned to read and count in German. By the 1920s and 30s the children were mostly unfamiliar with the German language. She remembers her parents laid a quilt on the floor with pillows, dishes and more pillows and then tied the four corners together and put them in the wagon for the journey to the campground. Opal states that her parents met at the campmeeting and that it was a time when courting began, and one made new acquaintances and friends. Most people really dressed up for the last Sunday Service. "That was dress up season," she states.

Left to Right: George Ratje, George Mahnken, Louis Kahrs, Frank Culbertson.

Clara Lindemann remembered when sheets were hung to divide the cabins and white tablecloths were placed on the table. The lofts were filled with straw and covered with quilts. Parents were afraid of children falling so the younger children slept on the ground level with the women. The best quilts were used to show off to friends. The kitchen was off to the side or in a lean-to at the back of the cabin in most of the cabins.

Rev. E. L. Rathert was the pastor in the 1940's at Lake Creek and in a 1961 interview explained: "The campmeeting used to be more of a revival meeting but over the years it has evolved into a week long prayer meeting in which we all give thanks." He evidently had some information about the early days of the campmeeting that we do not possess today. He explained that twenty persons gathered under a brush arbor in 1843 to begin the Lake Creek Campmeeting near where the Lake Creek Cemetery is now. It grew and people built little shanties around the area and stayed all week for the meeting. Rev. Rathert added: "The most people we had when I was here was about 500 but I know there were more before my time .... People seem to think they are busier now and don't have time for this kind of thing."

Nine ministers:—New campgrounds.
Front: —?—, —?—, Rev. D. W. Smith, Rev. Gustav Meyer;

Standing: —?—, Rev. Zwingli Meyer, —?—, Rev. E. C. Paustian, and Rev. W. C. Wagner.

Earl S. Lugen in 1961 remembered his 70 plus years of coming to campmeeting. He said he will never get tired of it. The climax that week he said was when ten children came forward to join the church. Then Rev. Linus Eaker charged each youngster with their responsibilities as the parents of the children stood behind them. Then the congregation left the tent and went to the church to honor the Rev. E. L. Hobbs, a retired minister that had spoken that morning. The women had prepared a noon day meal.

Dale Montgomery was born in 1942 and remembers his family cabin being very run down but in 1949 they remodeled it so some could stay in it. He remembers patches on the tent. The evening services always began with about 30 minutes of singing and always ended with an altar call.

No remembrances or insights would be complete without some reference to the German Heritage of Music at the Campground. Following are some German Campmeeting Songs:

HALLELUJAH

Hallelujah, Hallelujah,
Wir sind auf de reise Heim
Hallelujah, Hallelujah,
Wir sind auf de reise Heim

    Jesus, Jesus. Brunn des Lebens
    Stell ach stell Dich bei uns ein.
    Dasz wir jetzund nicht vergebens.
    Wirken und beisammen sein.

    Herr wir tragen deinem namen.
    Herr wir sind in Dich getauft
    Und Du hast, hast zu deinem samen
    Uns mit Deinum Blut erkauft.

The translation into English is:

Hallelujah, Hallelujah,
We are on the journey home.
Hallelujah, Hallelujah,
We are on the journey home.

    Jesus, Jesus, Well of Life
    Place, ah place yourself with us.
    That we now will not yield
    Work and be together.

    Lord, We carry your name
    Lord, We are in you baptized.
    And you have to your descendants
    Bought us with your blood.

Another well known tune used today as well as then is the Doxology, or Praise God from whom all blessings flow.

    Preist Gott, der alle segen giebt
    Preist Ihn, ihr menshen die Erlic,
    Ihr Himmelscore, alle preist,
    Den Vater, Sohn, und Heil'gen Geist.

The Cloud of Witnesses 53

Hallelujah

Those who have served and loved the Lake Creek Campmeeting over the years are truly a great cloud of witnesses for us. They blessed us with their presence, their time and their talents, and poured themselves into a Christian program which transmitted values of God's love to their families and to children yet unborn.

Front: Rev. Ernest Crepin, —?—, Rev. D. W. Smith, —?—, —?—;

Standing: —?—, —?—, —?—, Rev. Zwingli Meyer, Rev. Gustav Meyer.

54 *Chapter IV*

Group picture of German Methodist Pastors at Lake Creek, about 1893-94.
Front: Herman Koepsel, J. G. Kost, Henry Fiegenbaum, Charles Ott, J. J. Eichenberger, John C. Meyer, and Fr. Hauszer;

Back: H. H. Hackmann, Daniel Walter, John Demand, F. H. Wipperman, Alexander Fuhrman, J. H. Dreyer, J. H. Asling, J. A. Reitz, John A. Kracher, John Haller and Fr. Kaltenbach.

Chapter V
THE OBEDIENT ONES

From the inception of my dream of writing a history of the Lake Creek German Methodist Episcopal Church and Campmeeting, or, now, in the joint effort of actually doing it, an appropriate title seemed to be "The Obedient Ones." My reasoning came from the study of the many men who pastored the Osage Mission, later the Versailles Mission and finally the Lake Creek Church.

They didn't enter into the work of pastoring because no other work was available to them. They were called. Jacob Feisel was a brewmaster before he became a circuit riding preacher. Charles Stueckemann learned the carpentry trade before he became a preacher. J. George Schatz was born to Catholic parents. Sebastian C. and Philip Barth served as representatives of the American Tract Society before either of them entered the ministry. Daniel Walter's mother died when he was six; he attended school only occasionally, and he had to earn his own way among strangers until he was thirteen years of age. Herman Koepsel was confirmed in the Lutheran Church before becoming a Methodist. Gottlob J. Jaiser's father insisted that he become a blacksmith. He was obedient to his father's wishes, but the Lord led him elsewhere.

After these men conceded, sometimes reluctantly, to the Lord's leading, they endured more hardship because of the unsettled condition of the country. Jacob Feisel as early at 1849 described the Lake Creek vicinity as a "jungle", where his children did not see other human beings for weeks at a time . . . and were afraid of them when they did see them. Conveyances were almost nonexistent, there being only one wagon within a fifteen mile radius. If there was a stream of running water within fifty feet of their dwelling, that was a convenience. The conditions under which they lived were primitive and often life-threatening. But they endured; they persevered. And because of the deprivation they suffered, I today am able to live a comfortable life of ease and worship my Lord in the comfort of a church that insulates me from extreme heat and cold, a church where I can secure a drink of cool water or wash my hands with warm water . . . without ever leaving the building. And we worship the same God.

They were the true pioneers. They carved this wilderness into a habitable place. In spite of their seeming reluctance to accept their calling, in spite of the extreme hardships they endured, they didn't consider themselves deprived. It was part of their lives, and they lived them with a zest and a determination that any of us would do well to emulate. They were the Obedient Ones.

> A dirge for the brave old pioneer,
> A dirge for his old spouse;
> For her who blest his forest cheer;
> And kept his birchen house.
> Now soundly by her chieftain
> May the brave old dame sleep on;
> The red man's step is far away,
> The wolf's dread howl is gone.

Dorothy A. Bass
Smithton, Missouri
January 29, 1993

LUDWIG S. JACOBY

L. S. Jacoby was the first Presiding Elder over Lake Creek and sent the first preachers. He was born October 21, 1813, three days after the great battle of Leipzig, in old Strelitz, Mecklenburg, and died June 21, 1874 in St. Louis after a lingering and painful disease. He was of Jewish extraction with his father from the tribe of Levi and his mother also from the priestly line. Both parents were pious, God Fearing people, who with earnestness and deep solicitation prayed for their children that they might find grace before God and men. Young Jacoby had a pleasant childhood, received a good education, especially in the ancient languages, and would have received a thorough classical education had the means of his father permitted it. In 1835 he was baptized by a Lutheran clergyman. The Testament which he received from the minister and the earnest prayers of his parents laid the foundation for his later conversion. In 1839 he came to Cincinnati as a physician and later devoted himself to teaching English. On Christmas Day he attended a service and heard Dr. William Nast preach. The next week at watch night services he was converted and joined the Methodist Episcopal Church. Dr. Nast and a Brother Schmucker urged him to enter the ministry.

Ludwig Jacoby, First official German Missionary to Missouri.

In August of 1841 he was sent by Bishop Morris to St. Louis to begin a German Mission, the first in Missouri. He became a presiding elder in 1844 and was in charge of the preachers for the Lake Creek area.

In the year 1849 he felt the call to do something for his homeland. The Missionary Board agreed with him and sent him to Germany with instructions to begin his work in Bremen. After a successful 22 years there he returned to St. Louis where he pastored and served as Presiding Elder until his death in 1874.

FRANCIS HENRY WALKENHORST

"A circuit-riding preacher named 'Walkenhorst'" . . . he came in out of the mists into the jungle that comprised Pettis and Benton counties and then vanished into the mists in a couple of short years.

He left no footprints. He espoused no causes. He authored no books. He wasn't ordained. At frequent intervals, I wondered if he was a figment of my imagination. The Lake Creek Methodists knew of his existence, and the Lake Creek Lutherans confirmed his existence . . . but still there were no footprints. He didn't even have a first name . . . until two months ago.

My idle rummaging in my workroom one evening led me to volume 1 of the *History of Benton County*, Missouri by White and Miles. A number of years ago, Kathryn Kuhlman wrote me that she had no circuit-riding preachers in her ancestry . . . and I believed her. She just didn't know that her great-grandfather was the one I was seeking.

Credit should be given to Francis H. Walkenhorst for pointing out to the settlers in the Lake Creek areas of Pettis and Benton Counties that their corporate need for a church and a fellowship of believers was of great importance. Francis remained in this area only two years. He was born at Bielefeld, near Hanover, Germany, on November 5, 1810.* He was married in Hamilton County, Ohio on July 29, 1839 by "P. Schmucker," a minister of the gospel.* This was the Peter Schmucker who was a vital part of early Methodism in that area. Francis was then drawn into this central Missouri region.* (His wife, Mary W. Regeness, had been born September 22, 1809 in Hanover, Germany.)

Francis H. Walkenhorst performed only two marriage ceremonies in this area before moving on. Both are recorded in the Benton County Courthouse at Warsaw, Missouri. The first ceremony was the marriage of John Timpken to Katherine Behrens on November 29, 1840; the second was the marriage of Gerhard Ringen to Adelheid Timpken on December 20, 1840. Francis identified himself as a "Minister of the Gospel," though, at the time, he was not ordained as a Lutheran or a Methodist preacher.

After he left the Pettis/Benton County area, he moved to Lafayette County, the Concordia area, for it is there that his children were born: Elizabeth Magdalena, Sarah C., William Frederic, Rhoda Ann (married a Kretzmeyer), John Heinrich married Amelia Stoll) and Jacob W. Walkenhorst.*

William Frederic Walkenhorst, son of Francis, married Hannah Mathilda Kuester, and they had six children: Belle (married T. H. Nolte); Emma (married Joseph A. Kuhlman); Alberta (married Arthur Lipscomb); Ida; Pearl (married Francis S. Dilley); and Grant. Emma Walkenhorst married Joseph A. Kuhlman, and they became the parents of Kathryn Kuhlman of Evangelistic fame. Kathryn truly did not know that her great-grandfather began his career as a circuit-riding preacher in our central Missouri area!

During the Civil War, son William Frederic Walkenhorst served in Company A of the 7th Missouri State Militia; and in Company B and in Company D at various times; his father Francis was a member of the Home Guards.* On October 10, 1864, in a clash with bushwhackers, Francis Walkenhorst was one of those killed. Both Francis and his wife Mary are buried in Zoar Cemetery west of Concordia.

So ends the mystery of "a circuit riding preacher named 'Walkenhorst.' " His name is Francis, and he urged a new way of life on the people who listened to him. In 1843, a number of my German ancestors became charter members of the Lake Creek Methodist Episcopal Church located 7 miles south of Smithton, Missouri . . . the home church of five generations of my family. He made ready the path for Sebastian C. Barth, the first appointed circuit-riding preacher to our Versailles Mission.

---

*Census records and other information provided to the author by Homer Ficken and Ms. Buddy Samuels.

SEBASTIAN C. BARTH

Sebastian C. Barth was born near Frankfort in Hesse-Darmstadt, Germany on October 12, 1815, the middle son of five born to Sebastian Barth and his wife.

Sebastian Barth crossed the ocean in 1831 to seek a home in the New World, bringing with him a wife and five sons born to his former marriage; the mother of the sons had died in Germany.

The first settlement of the Barth family was at Chambersburg, Pennsylvania, but later on, Mr. Barth moved to Bedforth, Pennsylvania, and in 1837 came to Indianapolis, Indiana, among the early settlers of the city. He died soon after his arrival and the widow and sons were left to make their way in what was practically a new country. The two older sons were Adam, born in 1810, and George, born in 1813. These young men were successfully engaged in business in Louisville, Kentucky when their father died. They then came to Indianapolis and took the widow and the remaining children back with them to Louisville.

**Sebastian C. Barth
1843-1845.**

The family were what might be termed natural musicians. For a number of years, they traveled through the South giving concerts. Sebastian C. Barth was the third son, Philip the fourth, and John, the youngest. Of their father's second marriage, two daughters were born, Catherine and Elizabeth.

All the members of this family became converted and led worthy Christian lives. Adam enlisted in the Union army during the Civil War and suffering a sunstroke while in the service, died at his home in 1865. George raised a company at Louisville, was chosen captain, made a fine record at the front and was promoted several times, attaining the rank of colonel. When he died at his home in Louisville years later, he was buried with military honors. George was an ardent Republican. Philip, who became a minister, passed away at Iowa City, Iowa in the early 1900s. John, also a prominent clergyman, died at his home in Indianapolis. The sisters lived in Louisville. All the brothers except Sebastian C. were members of the Methodist Church when they died.

In 1840, Sebastian C. Barth was converted and united with the church. He gave up all worldly pursuits and devoted his life to the service of the Lord. His honorable and useful career, his unselfish spirit and devoted labors in the church attest to the sincerity of his vows of consecration. He and his brother Philip traveled as colporteurs of the Methodist Church in 1842 and 1843. In 1843 he entered the ministry of the Methodist Church at the request of the authorities of that body, having exhibited marked ability while exhorting during his work as a colporteur.

His first charge was the Versailles Mission, from Lexington to the mouth of the Osage River, twenty miles below Jefferson City, Missouri. He preached to the Germans under Presiding Elder Jennison, receiving a salary of fifty dollars a year.

Fifteen congregations were organized by him in the different counties, and the discharge of his duties involved a journey of three hundred miles on horseback every three weeks. During the first year, he used up three horses, which were given him by a kind Christian farmer. He would ride nights to reach his preaching point, often making a journey of fifty miles between sunset and sunrise.

Sebastian C. Barth married September 30, 1844 to the worthy and faithful helpmate who was his companion in life, Elizabeth Fieser, a native of Hasslock, Rheinpfalz, Germany. He rode the circuit in the Versailles mission only through 1845 because his young wife's health was delicate, and she did not like the isolation of the area. Otilie Maria Barth was born in 1845 and christened on October 20, 1845 in Cole County, Missouri. She was born to them in the Missouri wilderness.

Soon after his marriage, Mr. Barth was appointed by the Conference as pastor at Burlington, Iowa, where he remained two years. He was successively in charge at Quincy, Illinois; St. Louis; Wheeling, West Virginia; Pittsburg; Cincinnati; Lafayette, Indiana; Ann Arbor, Michigan; Toledo, Ohio; and Fort Wayne, Indiana. On account of throat trouble, he removed to Nashville, Tennessee where he remained from 1858 to the start of the Civil War in 1861. As his support was cut off because of war troubles, he came back to Indianapolis on the advice of his brother John. Here he found a prejudice against him because he had been connected with the Methodist Church South, and for six years—from 1861 to 1867—he was rejected, though he applied each year for an assignment as pastor.

Accordingly, in 1867, by an urgent invitation, he entered the Indiana Classis of the Reformed Church where he was engaged for forty years as an able and consecrated minister. He was in the Methodist ministry for twenty-four years, making in all sixty-four years during which he has preached the Gospel with singleness of mind and sincerity of purpose.

For three years, Mr. Barth was pastor of the First German Reformed Church in Indianapolis. He had charges in New Albany, Fort Wayne and Middletown, Indiana, and then, coming back to Indianapolis, took up mission work at Haughville and Springdale. In this work, he was engaged until 1895, when he resigned on his eightieth birthday. He and his wife with their two youngest daughters lived at 715 North West Street, Indianapolis. Reverend and Mrs. Barth had ten children, nine of whom lived, five sons and four daughters. Seven married and had families of their own. Mr. and Mrs. Barth, by their long marriage, were a beautiful illustration of ideal marital happiness. They celebrated their golden wedding in 1904—a privilege vouchsafed to few.

The fiftieth anniversary of the entrance of Mr. Barth into the ministry—1843 to 1893—was observed with loving zeal in 1893, the many friends of this aged and beloved servant of God making it a time of rejoicing and congratulation. It was first celebrated in the Brightwood congregation, all the Reformed churches in the city taking part, along with their respective ministers who addressed the large assembly of jubilaum. It was a great anniversary feast in honor of his fifty years' service in the ministry—a glorious time, to the honor of God through Christ the beloved Savior. The anniversary was also fittingly celebrated by the Hope Congregation at Springdale.

The anniversary of the Versailles Mission was also celebrated in 1893-94. Sebastian C. Barth in *Souvenir* states that he was privileged to attend the fifty year anniversary of the founding of the Mission at Lake Creek.

Mr. Barth prizes very highly a copy of *Souvenir of the West German Conference*, which was presented him by a committee of students and a professor of the Central Wesleyan College in Warrenton, Missouri. The Professor, as their president, wrote him a letter March 19, 1906, asking for information about the German Versailles Mission of which he was the first missionary, organizing congregations in 1843 and 1844. It was placed under the care of the West German Conference, but no member of the conference had any knowledge of the beginning of the mission except Mr. Barth, to whom, as first pastor, the Professor turned when appointed by a committee to write a church history, from the beginning, of every congregation under the care of said conference. Mr. Barth complied with his request for information concerning the mission, and was subsequently favored with a copy of the completed work.

Though he had lived in the United States since 1831, he still spoke German with much greater ease than English and evidently did his thinking in his mother tongue. This was evidenced by a question he put to a newspaper reporter, the form of the question, though in English, was distinctively German and marked by genuine German politeness: "Would you," he asked, "be so kind as to give me your very honorable name?"

Sebastian C. Barth retired from the ministry of the German Reformed Church in Indianapolis in 1895. With the exception of defective hearing, he retained at that time all of his faculties and was interested in all that was going on in the world. He came to this country in 1831 with his parents, landing at Baltimore, where his education was completed as far as schooling was concerned, and his subsequent acquirements came through reading and personal application to study without teachers.

During an interview with Mr. Barth by *The News*, he related the events of his life:

> We landed at Baltimore from Bremen on the fourth day of July, and it took us forty-two days in a sailing vessel to cross the ocean—a trip now made in one-sixth of that time. We settled on a farm at Chambersburg, Pennsylvania. My father was a musician with five sons. He and four of his sons, myself among the number, traveled over the country, especially through the South, giving concerts. I played the clarinet, trombone, violin and some other instruments. I was a musician for about eleven years and then entered the ministry of the Methodist Episcopal Church, preaching German. I rode a Missouri Circuit, covering 300 miles on horseback. This trip required three weeks, and in the summer, I usually traveled at night, going from Versailles to Lexington, Missouri, and taking in intermediate places. Many and many a time have I had to swim my horse over streams where there were no bridges. It was my business to visit the German settlements and speak to the settlers in their native tongue. I was in this missionary service for two years.
>
> .... In 1852, I went to Yellow Springs, Ohio, my health having broken down. For years, I was superannuated. Then I took up my work again.....

My family and myself were at Nashville at the breaking out of the Civil War. It was necessary to leave, and we came to Indianapolis in 1861. That was not my first sight of this place, however. I rode through it in 1837 when it was a village. I remember there was a blacksmith shop on the corner now occupied by the Claypool Hotel.

On coming to Indianapolis, I was invited to take pastoral charge of the German Reformed Church. The church was then in the middle of the square in Alabama Street, facing the Courthouse. I held that charge three years, having separated from the Methodist connection. I lived in this city then continuously until 1878, when I went to southern Indiana and had pastorates at Corydon, Crothersville and other places. Three years later, I returned to this city, which has since been my home. After my return until 1890, I had mission work at Brightwood, Haughville and Springdale on East Tenth Street.

Reverend Sebastian C. Barth, within weeks of becoming ninety-seven years old, died September 15, 1912 at the home of his daughter, Mrs. Henrietta McHolme, 1109 West 31st Street, Indianapolis. (Mrs. Barth died in 1908 at the age of eighty-six.) He had been ill with malarial fever for two weeks, but death was due to the infirmities of his extreme age. Interment was at Crown Hill Cemetery in Section 47, Lot 504. The pioneer circuit riding preacher of the Versailles Mission had ridden home.

HEINRICH NUELSEN

Heinrich Nuelsen was born in the North near Gottingen in the former Kingdom of Hannover on April 3, 1826, and according to the family register of his father, he was baptized in the Catholic church there three days later. He was educated as a Catholic and after several years, had the honor to mass-server. Although the parents were good Catholics, the light of the gospel came through in the family. The teacher in the town was namely a Lutheran, and through him, a brother of Heinrich Nuelsen was inspired to do the same. He soon became a pupil in the Barmer Mission House. During his visits to his parents' home, he brought Biblical books and tracts with him and made the gospel known to his brother. Although the father was upset about the direction his son was going, these visits always brought the family blessing. Leaving the family with the older children, the oldest son, Franz Nuelsen, traveled to America.

Heinrich Nuelsen
1844-1845.

He was converted to God as one of the first fruits of German Methodism in America through the work of Dr. William Nast in Cincinnati, and when he came to

Chapter V

Germany on a visit in the fall of 1841, he was a blessing to the family in that Heinrich, his brother, 15 years old, was led to the Lord in Cincinnati. Amalie Nuelsen, who had already earlier emigrated to America and was converted to God in Cincinnati, married Preacher L. S. Jacoby. He came with his young wife from St. Louis to Cincinnati in order to greet the parents on their arrival in the new homeland. Heinrich Nuelsen returned with his brother-in-law to St. Louis. There, he joined the existing congregation of only fourteen members. The sixteen-year-old Heinrich Nuelsen supported Br. Jacoby in the first German school which his brother-in-law had opened. Later, he undertook himself to head a second day school which Rev. Jacoby had founded in St. Louis. As schoolmaster, the young Nuelsen took care to announce to his fellow-workers the Word of God. When one remarked, "He is so young," Br. Jacoby secured for him an "Admonisher's License" and in September, 1844, took him on trial to the Missouri Annual Conference . . . at the age of eighteen. He was sent at once to the Illinois Conference with twelve other German preachers.

In 1844, the division namely took place, which the Southern Methodist Episcopal Churches led, and the German preachers did not want, as they said, to belong to the "Slavery Churches." Br. Nuelsen was added as an aide to the Preacher Sebastian Barth, who was head of the Versailles District, and had to serve the work-area almost completely alone for the head preacher was hindered from travel because of the bad illness of his wife. The District contained sixteen congregations which lay in a circuit of 250 miles. "In the backwoods region, the preacher could use no coach. It was, therefore, necessary to ride from one village to another on a horse. God sent his young disciple much success in his work. At the close of the conference year, some 100 people had joined the church."

In the next year, Br. Nuelsen was sent to a completely new area near Weston, on the western edge of the State of Missouri. He soon had ten preaching places in a circuit of 150 miles. At that time, St. Joseph was a small settlement of only a few hundred residents, and Br. Nuelsen gave the first German sermon in this city. At the end of the year, he could report a congregation of 50 awakened members in this district.

In order to go to the meeting of the Illinois Conference in Paris in the summer, the young preacher had to travel through the whole state of Missouri and through Illinois from the west to the east, which took fourteen days. he was ordained a deacon by Bishop Hamline and sent to Beardstown with the instructions to found a day school there. Here he then led, with the exception of Sunday evening, school every day from 8-12 and from 2-4, and rode in the evenings to the preaching places. As in the previous two years, his salary was seventy-five dollars, and out of this he had to pay for the subsistence of his horse. In Beardstown, the administrators paid his and his horse's costs with the school's money, and what was left over was applied to the chapel debt. The fourth and fifth years took him to Galena, Illinois. There he found a new chapel under construction and a total of five members, three of whom he soon had to throw out. Here, his salary was very small. In Burlington, where he was transferred in 1849, his work was so unsuccessful he asked the District Elder to transfer him. But he had to go back for a second year, and there emerged a fine awakening. Here in March, 1851, the call came to him to go as a missionary to

Germany and to report with Br. L. S. Jacoby in Bremen to the superintendent. In April of the same year, he landed in Bremen Harbor.

His works in Europe were also richly blessed. He was first preacher of the Bremen congregation and had to serve some twelve preaching places. In Bremen Harbor, he preached to the emigrants who always traveled in large numbers in the service of God. He did the same when he was transferred to Hamburg. As preacher in Frankfurt-on-the-Main, he had a large district over all and had to make long journeys. He came in the Pfalz, in Elias, in the Rhine province, to Wurtemberg.

After a richly blessed activity in Ludwigsberg, Br. Nuelsen was transferred in 1862 to Oldenburg in Grossherzogtum. Here, his wife, Magdalene Reuter, whom he had married in Galena, Illinois, died. In Oldenburg, he entered into marriage again with Rosalie Mueller, who outlived him.

In 1864, he became head elder of the Baseler District and worked in this position in rich blessing. Under his leading in Zurich, many were converted to God. From 1870 to 1874, he was in Basel again and from 1874 to 1877, he was active in Lenzburg, Kanton Aargau. As head elder, he worked from 1877 to 1883, partly in Frankfurt and partly in the Wurtemberg District, until the Fall of 1883 when he was called to be Director of the Book Company in Bremen. In 1889, he returned to America after he had dedicated thirty-eight years of his life to the work in Germany and Switzerland. He retired in 1891 in St. Louis, but died in Cincinnati, Ohio on August 19, 1911. One son, John L., became a Methodist Bishop.

HERMAN MAHNKEN

Herman Mahnken was born May 8, 1826 in Wilstedt, District of Ottersberg, Kingdom of Hannover, Germany. His early years were spent under the supervision of a Lutheran pastor. At the age of seventeen, he and his parents left Germany and came to America.

After spending a short time in New Orleans, he came to Missouri. As an honest farmer, he won the love and admiration of neighbors and businessmen with whom he came in contact. Father Mahnken spent his time not only in the accumulation of earthly treasures, but he had a spiritual vision which enabled him to reach out and lend a helping hand to those who were concerned about their soul's salvation. He came to America as a moral young man, but it did not last long. He soon realized he would have to renew his belief, and finally, after a hard battle, he received victory on December 25, 1844.

**Herman Mahnken
Lay Preacher.**

After he joined the Methodist Church, he was licensed as an Exhorter, and shortly after that, a Local Preacher's License was granted him. Later on, he was ordained a Local Preacher. His work as a Local Preacher was appreciated by many, and many a spiritual seed was scattered which will show its fruit when all things shall become known.

Herman Mahnken was one of the first to join Lake Creek after its organization. As a young man, he preached every other Sunday while the appointed minister filled other appointments in the circuit. In all, he preached more than fifty years.

On January 16, 1846, he married Margarete Ficken, and their marriage was blessed with four daughters and six sons. The wife, a son and a daughter preceded him in death.

For sometime, he was unable to get away from home because of the feebleness of his age; however, his strength still permitted him to go about the house and also to enjoy the presence of company until shortly before his death on December 23, 1917.

CONRAD RINGEN

Conrad Ringen was born February 11, 1803 in Germany. At an early date, he was married. In 1840, he married Margaretha —— Miller, widow of Claus Miller. Margaretha was born July 11, 1804 in Glenzstatt, Seven, Hannover, Germany. (Her previous husband, Claus Miller, died in 1839 in Covington, Kentucky. She had come to America with him in 1837.)

At the death of Claus Miller, Margaretha was driven, because of her great poverty and trouble, to the Lord, and she was converted that same year. At that time, she joined the church under the efforts of Dr. Wilhelm Nast in Cincinnati, and she then made her home with the families of the Brothers Zwahlen, Jacoby and Nuelsen. (Reverend Henry Miller, child of her first marriage, was a member of the St. Louis German Conference.)

Conrad Ringen was one of several "supply" preachers, i.e., lay pastors at Lake Creek. He had traveled for many years under the direction of the Presiding Elder, finally settling at Lake Creek. (When in the St. Louis area, he was a member at the Benton Street Church.) When he and his wife settled at Lake Creek, they became the first members of the church, and he continued his work as a lay preacher.

Conrad Ringen died on September 9, 1866, and Margaretha died November 23, 1893. Conrad is buried in the Lake Creek Cemetery, and Margaretha is buried in the Smithton Cemetery.

KONRAD EISENMEYER

Konrad Eisenmeyer is described as "an unassuming smart person who had good judgment and clear presentation." As a beginning pastor in September, 1845, he was assigned to serve Lake Creek and the remainder of the Versailles Mission. Records at Lake Creek indicate that he served for two years until 1847. In September, 1848, he was appointed Presiding Elder of the Wisconsin District.

WILLIAM SCHRECK

William Schreck was born in Lower Prussia, near Osnabrueck.

When yet young, in his native country, he was, through the instrumentality of Reverend Mr. Banning, awakened, but was not converted until he came to this country. In the vicinity of Pittsburgh, Pennsylvania at a campmeeting held by the English brethren, he was translated from the power of darkness into the Kingdom of God's dear son. During the labors of Brother Kisling, in Richmond, Indiana, he united with the Methodist Episcopal Church, and in the fall of 1842, he was received on trial in the Indiana Conference and under Brother L. S. Jacoby, who was then laboring in St. Louis, Missouri, he acted as a supply.

He labored as an itinerant minister thirty-two years with true self-denial and holy consecration, and God blessed his efforts with remarkable success. Following are his fields of labor: As Brother Jacoby's supply, he founded the Herman Mission; from thence, he was sent to the so-called "Lead Mines" Mission, now Galena and Dubuque; then Quincy, Milwaukee, St. Louis, Versailles Mission (now Lake Creek Circuit), Boonville, Missouri District (as Presiding Elder), St. Joseph, Leavenworth, Weston, Herman (for the second time), Mascoutah, Belleville District (as Presiding Elder), Highland, Columbus, Bushnell, Warren Circuit, And finally, Herman for the third time. This being his first field of labor and also, by the Lord's counsel, his last.

William Schreck
1847-1848.

He was described as a pious, liberal, energetic, practical man and a fond friend of children. He loved the doctrines and discipline of his Church and, indeed, all its institutions. On Sunday, March 22, 1874, he, in God's providence, finished his toils. In the evening of that day, his illness first became serious, though at that time, he did not realize his condition. But he had already expressed his readiness for the solemn hour of death, and with deep emotions, he praised the mercy and grace of the blessed heavenly Father. He died at the age of 58 from inflammation of the lungs on March 30, 1874.

HEINRICH C. DREYER

H. C. Dreyer was one of the first German pioneers of the West. He was born in 1816 and entered the ministry in 1845. His first appointment was Galena, Illinois in 1845. He then was sent to Jefferson City.

In 1848, he was appointed to Lake Creek, but served only one year, not unusual in those days. A photograph of Reverend Dreyer and his family standing in front of the log cabin church/parsonage at the present cemetery location appears elsewhere in this publication.

It appears that in 1849, Reverend Dreyer was sent from the Versailles Mission to St. Louis. At that time, his wife made this entry in her journal:

After our few belongings were packed at Versailles, we began our difficult journey. Part of the way our goods were transported on ox wagon. We sailed on the river at St. Louis; from there on the Mississippi and then further, it began to get dark. My husband walked into the city to find lodging while I sat with the sick child on the trunk. My husband did not return. The howling wind penetrated my whole body, while my heart was almost discouraged. He, however, could not find any rooms in the big city. A brother gave us one of his two rooms until my husband could build a parsonage. Lake Street was covered with planks. We could have neither wells nor cisterns. We bought water for six cents a barrel. Drinking water was very bad; cholera claimed many victims. Our oldest boy died also. Yet we are not discouraged if only souls can be saved.

What devotion—even in the face of discouragement, sickness and death!

He was appointed to Columbus Street in St. Louis; then Jefferson City a second time where he began preaching, but had to rest for three years to recover his health. When he again entered the ministry, he traveled to St. Joseph, Liberty, Oregon (Missouri), and Nebraska City and Omaha in Nebraska.

In 1862, the first German Campmeeting was held in Nebraska under the leadership of H. C. Dreyer. He later served Leavenworth, Kansas until 1866 when his health became so impaired that he had to take a superannuated relationship. Even so, he continued to preach and labor as much as his feeble powers permitted. He was an energetic minister and a diligent worker. In his early years, he proclaimed the message of reconciliation while denying himself proper nutrition and adequate rest. Because of this, and often times exposure to the extreme heat and cold weather, it is believed he laid the foundation to disease and his premature death on April 30, 1870.

JACOB FEISEL

Reverend Jacob Feisel was born on May 13, 1812 in Dodenau, Hessen-Darmstadt. He grew up in a quiet family circle of a gardener. He acquired the respect of his teacher and after his confirmation, he became a brewmaster. After this achievement, he came to the United States on June 3, 1834. During the journey, the ship had to endure many days of severe storm in which the formerly happy audience, under the jostling of the waves and the cracking of the masts, fell to their knees and promised God to serve Him if they could be allowed to reach the long-sought shore safe and sound.

After his arrival in Baltimore, Maryland on September 6, he was struck with a severe illness which lasted eighteen months. But he forgot to fulfill his promise when he was in despair. After several journeys, he arrived in the year 1839 in Beardstown, Illinois, where he read in the newspaper entitled *The Priest's Enemy* such horrible things about the Methodists that he made the promise "I'll stop their doings as soon as I have the occasion to do so." From that time on, he always kept them in his thoughts and whenever the Methodist name was mentioned, it enraged him.

Through the influence of Brother Heminghaus and Brother Kuhl, who later became successful preachers, and through the influence of his religiously motivated wife Luise Krause, many of his prejudices about this religion and about the Methodists disappeared, at the same time, however, upsetting his spiritual beliefs.

Jacob Feisel
1849-1850,
1852-1853.

In this frame of mind, he settled in Quincy, Illinois, where he found that his relatives had become Methodists. At the quarterly Conference, Dr. Jacoby had the evening service which left him with an impression, causing many to cry and continue to sob. "Even if everyone cries, I will not cry. Of that you may be sure. I would not become converted if the preacher thundered for fourteen days." During the Holy Scare, he decided on October 26, 1845 to become a member. At that time, al large change had come about. He now served the church in bringing other fellowmen the leaf of Christianity. Br. Heminghaus who served the Quincy community gave to him his license to preach. Only after a long fight and much persuasion by the brethren did he decide to enter the preaching profession. His first assignment was the Versailles Mission in Missouri. In order to reach this assignment, the family had to travel from the Missouri River twenty-five miles by oxcart, during which Sister Feisel became seriously ill. The parsonage was located in the area called Lake Creek—a small log cabin in the middle of the jungle. It had two rooms which were very low. When the preacher's wife cleaned the stove, she scared many snakes from their nests, and they slithered about the floors.

The Mission had 15 preaching places; the Missionary received a helper. They extended the preaching area to five counties up to the Kansas Border. When Br. Feisel left, Sister Feisel sometimes did not see a person for a week other than her children, who soon became shy of people. She used to say: "There I am like Robinson Crusoe on a lonely island." The new settlers lived in meager conditions and shared with the preacher's family what they could. The salary amounted to $160; they took in thirty people as new members and converted twenty-one during that year.

In the entire district circumference of fifteen miles, there was only one wagon, and a family had brought the same from Germany. When the settlers needed the barest necessities for the household, they loaded the wagon with meat and exchangeable products and with oxen, went to the 40-mile distant Boonville on the Missouri River, and from there, brought every neighbor his share. There were, however, wagons whose wheels consisted of large discs which were sawed off of a tree trunk. Such wagons made the impression from some distance of the wagon frame being moved on four large slices of cheese.

The members of the settlers sought their unconverted friends and neighbors who were usually converted. During one of these assemblies in the year 1849 came the wife of Johann Timken, whereupon he became so enraged that he stood up on the seat of the last bench, forcing his way to his wife, and tried to pull her down under the words, "Woman, do you want to come down?" That, however, thought Hermann Kahrs, a very strong man, was an intrusion into the personal rights of the wife, and he grabbed, therefore, the excited Timken so firmly by his throat that poor Timken's eyes stared skyward while Kahrs shouted at him, "John, will you be quiet? I will do nothing to you. I just want to ask you, don't you want to be quiet?" Whereupon, Timken became as peaceful as a lamb.

When Reverend Feisel's assignment in the Versailles Mission ended, he was assigned to the Brunswick Mission, which the previous preacher had left in the middle of the year due to a lack of food. At the Conference, he had inquired of the Superintendent, who gave him the laconical reply. "Go there; you will find the people." While he arrived at his destination, he was met at the yard of Mr. Modemeyer by a number of men whom he at once determined had been drinking something that left a different effect upon them than water. One with an exceptionally loose tongue asked, "Are you the new preacher of the Conference?" Mr. Feisel said, "Yes." The man said, "We were once Methodists, but we are not anymore. We have taken everything away—the church and what belongs to it. We do not want anything from the Conference any more." That caused the temple vein of the missionary to swell, and he replied in not-to-be-misunderstood words, "People, this you can take note of. I do not scare easily. The Conference has sent me here, and the Devil himself will not carry me away." After a short conference, the wise Gamaliel said, "That person has a pair of lightning eyes; we had better not pick on him." And everyone, therefore, went home.

During the previous pastor's absence, a Lutheran preacher named Hickman came to the people of the Brunswick circuit and by false representation, he acquired the congregation of the church, but Reverend Feisel's energetic appearance ruined their entire plan.

In the Brunswick circuit, the family had to endure much lack of wordly goods. The Missionary had only one suit, and the coat was made from a material which the sister of Mrs. Feisel in St. Louis had given to Mrs. Feisel for a dress.

The income during that year amounted to $150, and on that one had to exist. The house rent cost $60, and there was horse fodder and ferry expenses. "But God helped us to get past that, and we had a lot of enjoyment. A respectable number of former members congregated, and new ones were added. When the souls were saved, we were all well paid for our troubles and denial." How many preachers would today remain in the work field under such conditions?

The Versailles Mission was then dividend into four districts in 1851, and Reverend Feisel received the part which is called Florence District, where he received $225 in salary. "And during the two years, I recuperated with my family, again in earthly relation."

In the year 1853, he was appointed Presiding Elder of the St. Louis District, which he accepted with a heavy heart. This district was very large and had to be traveled by horseback. Some days, he sat in the saddle from morning to night and would eat his frugal meals on a log or in the grass while he would hold the horse by the reins while the horse grazed. Often, he would carry along some corn in a saddle bag, for in many places, there was no food for the horse. In Lexington, Missouri, he and a fellow preacher couldn't find any food for their horses. A widow, however, had a bucket full of bran for her cow, and we divided the same into three parts, and every horse received a bowl full. "I only do this," she said in an aloof tone, "because the gentlemen pastors and their horses should not go hungry." The next morning, the animals had to travel fifteen miles until they came to a brother where they could be fed properly. During the fourteen years in this district, 800 people joined the church and between 600 and 700 accepted Christ.

Since the Presiding Elder in those days received most of the books from the publishing house for preachers in Cincinnati, Br. Feisel personally sold to members and preachers of the St. Louis District about $1,230 worth of books. When the four years in the St. Louis District had expired, he was assigned to the Missouri District which encompassed 1,268 square miles, and most of that had to be traveled by horseback. Once it happened that he and Br. Schatz arrived in a new settlement in Nebraska, where they had no Inn or private house available to hold a service, and it was also too cold to hold it outdoors. Finally, a young man volunteered his uncompleted house of two rooms for the services. After the service, the preachers were not invited for dinner by anyone, for the people had only the barest food supplies and were embarrassed to offer some to the preachers. So, they remained with the bachelor who was thereby embarrassed and expressed his uneasiness in asking that they please shake the dust off of their feet and go. That is when Brother Feisel finally spoke up and said, "It seems that we shall be guests for dinner." Whereupon, the bachelor replied, "Oh, no. That is impossible. Where should I get a meal for the preachers? I have no wife." Through friendly encouragement, he finally fetched some potatoes, and Br. Feisel and Schatz took the peeling knife and began to peel the potatoes. That was too much for the bachelor, and he finally explained very definitely that the assistant preacher could, under the circumstances, peel the potatoes, but that the head preacher simply could not do that. They made a meal from potatoes, corn meal, and chicken, which the preachers finally enjoyed. During the three years, 425 people joined the truth; 200 acceptances were reported. Books from the publishing house amounted to $1,100. When the District was divided, he received the Kansas District and thereafter served in important fields in Missouri and Illinois and removed himself in 1881 from active duty due to narrow chest (probably asthma), and resided at Quincy, Illinois. He spent a nice retirement until May 16, 1895 when he passed away and joined the Lord.

Chapter V
The Personality of the Man

1. Br. Feisel was a very large, heavyset man whose nerves seemed to be as flexible as steel; therefore, he could stand extreme heat of the summer and the penetrating cold of the winter from early morning 'til late at night, riding in the saddle, and at nights sleeping in stalls and miserable huts without letting it affect his attitude and health.

2. He was an honest straight personality and always called things by their right name. He flattered no one, preferred no one over the other, and had no love for people who tried to carry water on both shoulders. Therefore, some people did not enjoy his presence or thrive on him. During a conversation, he would be friendly and educating. By nature, he was gifted with a large measure of human understanding and foresight and energy. It didn't take long for him to evaluate a person and seldom would he fail in his judgment. I remember many times that he gave a negative judgment about beginning preaching candidates and warned of their acceptance, and in every case, his judgment was accurate.

3. In the religion, he shied away from all formality and worldliness. He did not want to have his churches filled with worldly members and therefore, pressed for an acceptance of God. He led a debate in the *Christian Advocate* stating that acceptance by God, not catechism and Confirmation, was the Biblical law for acceptance into the church. Also, he kept strict order and discipline; his administration was, however, free of narrow-mindedness and undue harshness as the following examples will prove. When he was in an old community in Illinois as preacher, he was visited by several members, and at last searched out by the Board of elders who encouraged him to preach against the carrying of gold. He promised to investigate the matter. Several Sundays later, he began his sermon as follows: "I have been requested to preach on the carrying of gold, especially of that by the young feminine members. I have used this of these like Paulus of Athens and taken a personal survey, but to my great astonishment, I have found devilish little gold. What seems to be gold in most cases was gold covered bronze, and over that, surely nobody would want to get heated." That put an end to the matter.

In his sermons, he always moved on religious grounds and carried some in a practical way with clearness and warmth; therefore, the people enjoyed listening to him. Such remembrance remains his blessing. His death occurred May 16, 1895.

WILHELM NIEDERMEIER

At the Conference in September, 1848 under Bishop Morris in Belleville, Illinois, Wilhelm Niedermeier was welcomed as a new pastor and appointed to Weston, Missouri. In 1850-1851, he preached at Lake Creek and Florence, Missouri.

JOHN HAUSAM, SR.

John Hausam, Sr. preached at Lake Creek in 1851-52. He is listed in the *Souvenir of the West German Conference* as being a member of the Conference from 1851-53, 1856-57, and 1868. In 1851, he was a member of the Illinois Conference, and in 1857 the Southern Illinois Conference, pastoring at St. Joseph, Missouri. It is believed that he is the father of John Hausam, Jr. who preached at Lake Creek from 1880-84. A sketch of John Hausam, Jr.'s life appears later. While at Lake Creek, a daughter named Maria was born on December 23, 1851 to John Hausam, Sr. and his wife who was also named Maria.

According to *Souvenir*, John Hausam, Sr. was appointed a Presiding Elder in 1855-59 for the Missouri District of the German Conference.

John Hausam, Sr.
1851-1852.

PETER HELLWEG

Peter Hellweg was born March 13, 1817 at Assel, Hannover, Germany. He came in July, 1839 to New York; in the fall of 1840, he came to Marietta, Ohio. There he met Martha Danker, the daughter of Reverend George Danker, whom he married on November 12, 1841.

Since his wife was already converted, she attended an evening Watch Night service in 1841-42 at the church. Brother H. Koneke was the preacher, and everyone was inspired by his sermon. Peter went to the altar on invitation of the preacher, and when the song " 'How the Fog Must Disappear,' etc., was sung, the Morning Star lit up my heart at midnight," thus read his notation.

Peter Hellweg
1853-1855.

In April, 1843, Peter and Martha Hellweg came to German Creek, Iowa. Through a letter to Father Danker in 1844, a preacher named J. Mann came. Filled with love for his countrymen, he invited people to his house of God. Soon thereafter, Peter received a local preacher's license, and in 1847, he was sent out as a traveling preacher by Dr. L. S. Jacoby. The following assignments were listed in the Family Bible: Des Moines Mission, Farmington, Iowa and Missouri, 1847-49; Herman (church built), 1849-51; St. Joseph (church built), 1851-53; Lake Creek (church enlarged), 1853-55; Muscatine, Iowa, 1855-57; Burlington, Iowa, 1857-58; Rock Island, Illinois, 1858-60; Davenport, Iowa, 1860-61; Muscatine, Iowa, 1861-63; Sherrill's Mount, Iowa, 1863-66; Girard, Clayton County, Iowa, 1866-68; Colesburg, Delaware

County, Iowa, 1868-71; Liberty Ridge, Wisconsin, 1871-73; Plattsville, Wisconsin, 1873-74; York, Delaware County, Iowa, 1874-75.

Even if Peter Hellweg was not the most gifted speaker, he was an ambitious fire-and-brimstone preacher who converted many souls. His love of soul-saving and faithfulness regarding what was entrusted to him were his main character traits. The choice of his church was very dear to him, and the *Apologete* was essential. When the latter did not come on Thursday mornings, he inquired to see if others had received it. Whenever he read it, it gave refreshment to him. The most important articles were marked with a cross, and his dear ones would read those articles first. Thus, the last *Apologete* was also marked. He also read *Hearth and Home*. That, including the Bible and his sermon book, could not be spared to the end. Since Brother Hellweg could hardly hear at all in his last years, he, therefore, attended the church services little. His heart, however, remained warm for the holy work. As soon as anyone would enter the house on a visit, he would ask, "How is the community?" and tears would run down his cheeks in compassion. Whenever souls were converted, he would cry tears of happiness. And whenever he would relate experiences of earlier times, tears would accompany his words.

In the Fall of 1875, he had moved to a farm near Charles City, Iowa where he lived fifteen years alternately with his daughters. During his last years, he lived in Garner with his son-in-law Adam Schneider, where he died on February 5, 1897. When he tried to speak his last and unable, he pointed heavenward as if to say, "I'm going home."

HEINRICH LAHRMANN

Heinrich Lahrmann was born January 23, 1823 in Lintorf, District of Wittlage, Hannover, Germany.

On September 3, 1845, he traveled to America. He married Dorothea Stahlhuth on April 1, 1849.

On April 11, 1847, he joined the Methodist Church in St. Louis and was converted to God shortly after Pentecost. In 1849, he was sent to the Wash Street congregation to work in the vineyard of the Lord. He served two years in Springfield, Illinois, 1849-51; Chester, Illinois, 1851-52; St. Charles, 1852-54; Boonville, 1854-55; Florence (Lake Creek), 1855-57; Wash Street, St. Louis, 1857-58; St. Louis District 1858-62; Wash Street congregation, St. Louis, 1862-64; Quincy, Illinois District, 1864-68; Pekin, Illinois, 1868-71; Peoria, Illinois, 1871-72; Muscatine, Iowa, 1872-74; in 1874, he served as agent of the German College in Mt. Pleasant, Iowa; Warsaw, Illinois, 1875-78;——, St. Louis, 1878-81; Bloomington, Illinois, 1881-84; Mascoutah, Illinois, 1884-87; Keokuk, Iowa, 1887-91, forty-two years in all.

Heinrich Lahrmann
1855-1857.

Because of his hard suffering which came on him during his last Conference year, it was a time of special testing and purification. A few days before his death, after a trying time, he called out: "Mamma! Soon I go home, praise the Lord!" "Aren't you afraid of death, Papa?" Sister Lahrmann asked. He smiled a moment and answered: "Why should I be afraid? Jesus is here to fetch me. I have an unshakable faith in God. Heaven and earth will go away before any of His words. The grace of God is greater than sin, hallelujah!"

The Word of God, which he diligently read during his life, was now a source of rich comfort for him. Shortly before the end, after he was exhausted from a severe attack, he opened his arms and said: "Father, here I lie in your favor, only by grace. All is well, all is well. God be thanked that I could address my loving congregation last Sunday of the obedience of Abraham amidst his fear; God be blessed." Then to Sister Lahrmann he said: "It will be hard for you when I am gone and I cannot speak to you; but then, Praise God for my deliverance and hold fast to the faith; you will soon come, and I will be on the bank to receive you." After he awoke from a short nap, Sister Lahrmann asked him if he wished to say anything. "Yes!" he said. "Tell everyone to be clean from sin. Tell the children to remain obedient. I expect all of you in Heaven."

All of the children were called together at his request. When they stood around the bed, he blessed each one individually and then intoned the verse: "God be with you 'till we meet again." When the last battle finally came, he joined his hands, and one could hear him slowly pray: "God help me. O God help me—until the last moment." A few more minutes passed, and Brother Lahrmann had departed, blessed in the Lord on June 12, 1891 in Keokuk, Iowa. His wife, five daughters and two sons looked on longingly. Three sons and one daughter had preceded him in death. He is buried in the United Methodist Wesleyan Cemetery in St. Charles, Missouri near the intersection of Interstate 70 and Highway 94.

JACOB MAGLY

Jacob Magly was born March 8, 1821 at Steinweiler, Reinbaiern, Germany and came to America as a 15-year-old boy. At the age of twenty-one, he was converted through a sermon given by Father Koeneke. His conversion was the first at the old Race Street Church in Cincinnati, Ohio, where he lived for many years under the administration of Dr. Miller in union with Sisters Tantau and Theuerkaus, who had the right of membership.

April 4, 1844, he married Sister Margaretha Klippel and had ten children, of which six, four sons and two daughters lived.

Reverend Magly had served the church as a successful traveling preacher for nearly seven years, especially one year at Westport, Missouri, 1852-53; Brunswick, 1853-55; Dalton, 1855-57; Florence and Lake Creek, 1857-59; and Leavenworth, Kansas, 1860-62, where he built a church.

After that, he entered into the circle of stationary preachers. On May 24, 1889, he came to San Jose, California and became a faithful member of that community until he died of pneumonia on May 25, 1891. He was of high standing, enjoyed the words of God and listened to his teachings.

PHILIP HEHNER

Philip Hehner was born February 1, 1827 in Zimmerscheib on the Lahn River in Germany and came to St. Louis, Missouri in 1849, where he soon had influence in the German Methodist Church in Warrenton. Three years later, he became a preacher and did much frontier work in the West under great difficulty.

From *Souvenir of the West German Conference*, a partial listing of his assignments is found: Lake Creek, 1859-61; Arley, 1861-62; Columbus, 1864; Dalton, 1866-69; Corder and Lexington, 1875-77.

He retired after thirty-five years of active service. As a religious man, his motto was "Belonging entirely to the Lord."

From General Services Administration, Washington, D. C., it was learned that Philip Henna enlisted in the Missouri State Militia on September 20, 1861 and was assigned to the 3rd Battalion. In his application for a pension in July, 1890, he stated that he was affected by "nervous prostration to the extent of total disability to preach, that being his profession, and also rheumatism, also physical disability on account of age, the two first brought on from exposure in the service. In December, 1861, he had to lay and sleep in the snow about sixty miles east of St. Joseph, Missouri" and from that time on, he had to suffer with the rheumatism in the left shoulder and lower left arm. He was honorably discharged on July 11, 1862.

Philip Hehner
1859-1861.

He died on April 21, 1909 in a rest home in Quincy, Illinois and was buried at Warsaw, Illinois.

ANDREAS HOLZBEIERLEIN

Andreas Holzbeierlein, at the age of fourteen, came with his parents from Germany to America and stopped for a while in the New England States. Some time later, they crossed the Appalachian Mountains on horseback, making their way to the Cole County, Missouri vicinity.

About this time, Andreas met a friend whose acquaintance he had made in Germany, Father Dreyer (Heinrich C. Dreyer), a German Methodist circuit rider. Andreas was originally a Catholic, but was converted by Father Dreyer to Methodism.

Andreas eventually made his way to the Lake Creek, Missouri area, for on September 15, 1853, he married Adelheid Kahrs, who, at the age of four, along with her family, had settled in the Sedalia, Missouri vicinity. Andreas and Adelheid had nine children (four died in infancy): Emma M. (born April 20, 1864, married

Herman A. Sleyster), Henry, Lewis and John W. are the names of the ones known to me.

Andreas and Adelheid were some of the first white settlers to reside among the Indians In Wyandotte County. Following is a partial listing of his ministerial appointments: 1850-52, Oregon, Missouri; 1853, Weston, Missouri; 1855-56, Arley, Missouri; 1857-58, First Church in Kansas City, Kansas; 1858-59, Dalton, Missouri; 1862-63, Arley, Missouri; 1863-64, Lake Creek, Missouri.

Andreas and Adelheid moved to a farm at Pondcreek, Oklahoma, Oklahoma Territory, where he died of cancer on October 16, 1897. It is believed by family members that he is buried on the farm at Pondcreek, Oklahoma, but that Adelheid is buried in the Mount Hope Cemetery, Kansas City, Kansas. The cemetery adjoins the Quindaro Cemetery, which was part of the property owned by Andreas and Adelheid when they ministered in the Kansas City area.

CHARLES HENRY STUECKEMANN

Charles Henry Stueckemann was born in Lensingenhausen, Westphalen, Germany on April 27, 1828. His father died when he was yet young. When fourteen years of age, he was made an apprentice to learn the carpenter trade in the city of Muhlheim on the River Ruhr. After learning his trade, he came to the United States in July, 1848, and made Louisville, Kentucky his home. There he joined the Methodist Episcopal Church in March, 1849, during Father Danker's administration. On July 22 of the same year, he sought and received pardon of his sins and found peace in believing in our blessed Saviour Jesus Christ and obtained a lively hope of eternal life. As the church perceived his talent and was about to give him a license to preach, he left Louisville, traveling to and fro until finally he settled down in St. Joseph, Missouri. From there, he was sent to Brunswick, Missouri in 1857 to preach the glorious Gospel.

The following were his appointments: Brunswick; Fort Riley, Kansas; Wyandotte; Lawrence, Florence (Lake Creek), Missouri, 1864-66 (He performed the marriage ceremony of my great-grandparents Rages on April 27, 1865 near Pyrmont.); Alton, Illinois; Jacksonville, Pittsfield, Smithton and Sedalia, Missouri; Enterprise, Kansas; Kansas City, Missouri; Wathena, Kansas; and Pittsfield, Illinois. While at Lake Creek, Aron Dennis Stueckemann on April 7, 1864, was born to Charles and Margaretha Kohler-Stueckemann. He also became a Methodist preacher.

From *Souvenir*, it is learned that during the Civil War, courageous preachers carried on the work in a holy and masterly way. The first German Campmeeting in Kansas was held near Wathena, where the Columbus Home Guards kept order and the Rebels were kept away. In Lyons Creek in 1862, the first campmeeting was held with Pastors May, Muller and Stueckemann, Presiding Elder Steinley having charge.

Reverend Stueckemann died December 11, 1882 of paralysis in Pittsfield, Illinois.

J. GEORGE SCHATZ

J. George Schatz was born in 1829 of Catholic parentage at Wahlwies, Nassau. While still young, he put his trust in God and often received great peace directly from the Comforter while engaged in earnest prayer so that when he grew to riper years, the ceremonies and superstitions of his Church became as a dead-letter to him.

In 1849, he emigrated to America. In Looking-glass Prairie, Illinois, he found a home at the house of a truly pious Methodist family. The holy walk, the Christian family life, and the warm and practical sermons of Reverend W. Fiegenbaum convinced him soon that there was something in religion which he did not yet possess. He sought and found forgiveness of his sins in the blood of Christ on August 13, 1850 at a campmeeting. "Now I have received," he himself wrote, "a better absolution than any of the Popes were ever able to give."

In 1851, he received a license to exhort and served as a supply in Marthasville, Warren Mission and Vandalia. In 1853, he was received on trial in the Illinois Conference, and thereafter was appointed as follows: Union Circuit; Oregon, Missouri; Nebraska City; Wyandotte; St. Joseph District; Columbus; Brunswick; Lake Creek, 1867-69; Oregon, Missouri, where this plain but faithful servant of the Lord ended his earthly career in triumph.

While at Lake Creek, a daughter, Margaretha Elisabeth Schatz, was born on February 20, 1867 to J. George and Catherina Ortman-Schatz.

Reverend Schatz's last illness prostrated him so completely that it was almost immediately evident that human aid would be unavailing; but our brother was ready for either life or death. Only four days before the end he received such a revelation of God that he exclaimed, "never before had I thought that a mortal man could experience such a thing." Just before his death, his Presiding Elder asked him, "Brother, are you ready to die?" To which he replied, "O yes! Long ago." He died April 5, 1872 at Oregon, Missouri.

HEINRICH HANKEMEYER

Heinrich Hankemeyer was born in 1824 in Lippe-Detmold, Germany. When he was thirty years old, he traveled to America. Soon after that, he joined the Methodist Church, was converted to God and felt at the same time the call to preach the Gospel to his countrymen.

In 1853, he married Friedricke Meyer. This marriage was blessed with eight children, of which one son became a preacher of the Gospel in the Congregational Church. One son, Carl William Hankemeyer, was born to them on December 4, 1869 while they pastored Lake Creek.

In 1857, he was accepted into the Southern Illinois Conference and later, he joined the Southwest German Conference. He worked for twenty-four years as an active preacher and served during this time in the following districts: Alton, Illinois; Jackson, Missouri; Lake Creek, 1869-71; Drake, twice; Sedalia; DeSoto; Metropolis, Illinois; Bland, Missouri; Cape Girardeau; Mossiron; New Melle, Missouri; and Golconda, Illinois.

In 1880, he accepted a superannuated position in the St. Louis German Conference and lived after that in Hopewell, Missouri, where, during the next six years, his home burned and all of his valuable papers were lost. After this great loss, he moved to his children's in St. Louis, Missouri, but settled after a few years in Jonesburg, Missouri.

As a superannuated preacher, Reverend Hankemeyer had sold some Bibles and other Christian books at his previous charges, and so in his modest wisdom, he did much good. On one such visit to Drake, Missouri, he caught a cold that was so bad that he had to hasten his return home. However, one suspected nothing dangerous for he had sometimes had such illnesses. On November 8, 1896, he sat as usual in his chair and in the evening, went to bed; fifteen minutes later, he passed away quietly without a word said in the presence of his family.

JOHN PHILIP MILLER

John Philip Miller, a longtime member of the St. Louis German Conference, was born August 13, 1836 in Bremerhaven, Germany. He came in 1840 with his parents to America, first to St. Louis and then in the area of Jefferson City Missouri. Here he attended the public school and the Forest Hill Academy and then attended one year at the Methodist College in Quincy, Illinois. Because of a lack of money, he had to stop going to school and became a schoolteacher. At this time, he received his admonisher's license from Reverend Peter Hehner, and in 1858, he received his preaching license from Reverend Jacob Feisel and started in the active ministry in the same year. He entered on trial the Illinois Conference, and his first assignment was in Omaha, Nebraska.

His salary that year was $125 in Mission money. The next year, the conference sent him to Lawrence, Kansas. This Mission included Lawrence, Tecumseh, Topeka, Ballwin and the land in between. Here his salary was likewise $125.

On September 18, 1860, he married Mary W. Feisel. This marriage was blessed with six children. One, Phoebe Louise Miller, was born to them on July 21, 1872 while they were at Lake Creek.

Reverend Miller served the following churches: Boonville, Missouri, 1863; Lexington, Missouri and Freedom Kansas; Lawrence, Kansas, 1864; Lyona, Kansas (which included today's Enterprise); Junction City, Kansas, 1868-69; Lake Creek, Missouri, 1871-73; Smithton; St. Charles, 1876; St. Louis (Soulard Street; Springfield, Illinois; Davenport, Iowa; and Jones City.

He had to accept superannuation in 1879 because of lung trouble, and after he studied medicine, he devoted himself to the medical practice. During his last twelve years, he lived in Enterprise, Kansas, where he made himself useful and brought blessing to some. His wife died on February 24, 1911, and Reverend Miller died January 6, 1916.

LEONHARD GOTTFRIED HILMER

Leonhard G. Hilmer served the Lake Creek charge from 1873 to 1875. From 1875 to 1877, he was located at Dalton, Missouri. In 1879, according to the Commission on Archives and History of the United Methodist Church, Reverend Hilmer was a member of the Southwest German Conference but withdrew that year under charges according to the Conference minutes. He died in 1904.

WILLIAM FOTSCH

Reverend Fotsch wrote his own short life summary shortly before his admission to the hospital and subsequent death:

I was born October 8, 1847 at Unterhallau, Switzerland. In 1864, I came to Basel under the influence of the Christian Unity for Young Men, and I was confirmed to same March 4, 1866 and found a pearl of dear value.

From 1867-69, I was in a mission house, and on Easter, 1869 I landed in New York where I spent three further years in a preacher's seminar. In St. Louis, Missouri, I met Father Ellerbeck, and under the earnest prayers of Sister Ellerbeck, I was persuaded to become a Methodist. I joined the church, and from April to September became Charles Harms' helper at Peoria, Illinois. In 1872, I became a trial member of the St. Louis Conference. My first assignment was Brushhaven. In 1874, I married Sister Minna Hausmeier from Beardstown, Illinois. The Lord gave us six children, three of which died, one three-week-old daughter, one daughter twelve years old, and Emma, Mrs. Frederick Wolther, died at the age of thirty-one. Many are waiting for me above, Hallelujah! (Emma Maria Fotsch was born to them on September 3, 1876 while they pastored Lake Creek.)

From 1872-1905, thirty-three years, I tried with God's help to serve God and his people. The poor, sick and unfortunate have always encouraged me to live for God. This work offered me a great peace of mind. For twenty years I rode to DeSoto through the country. The horse shied and reeled backward. I fell and received an injury which caused me much pain. At the time, I ignored it, but when the pain returned ten years later and increased and I could not ride any more, I could hardly preach any more. In 1905, I felt it necessary to give up preaching, so I retired and lived in DeSoto, Missouri.

On Easter Sunday, 1910, I gave the Last sermon (text, Col. 3,1). Soon, thereafter, I felt severe pains in the stomach. I was very sick and suffered in the summer of 1910. In May of that year, I discovered a hard knot on my left side, and the Doctor identified it as a growth in the spleen. This encouraged me to go to St. Louis and have further X-rays. Dr. Du Holsten said that it was a very severe cyst. The abnormal swelling caused me much pain. This operation could now be life or death. God gave me much happiness during these days. I will also relate to you that I will go next Sunday to the Hospital. God may be blessed for Eternity. At least, it seemed to me as if many relatives smilingly held their hands down towards me, and I go gladly from believing to seeing. I thanked the Conference brothers for their love and help which they have given me. I just now heard that Brother Bosholl went home, whose district in 1873 was Des Moines, Iowa, and Brother Ott with whom I was ordained, and now lives with God 'til we meet again, and God may be thanked and praise all those who have given me forgiveness. My work has been done. I have nothing left to do on this Earth but to go to Jesus.

William Fotsch

Reverend Fotsch died July 17, 1910 at DeSoto, Missouri. Among my collection of obituaries previously in the possession of Aunt Anna Rages-Ringen was an obituary of Louise Wilhelmina Fotsch, daughter of William and Minna Fotsch. She was born April 28, 1882 in Rock Island, Illinois and died September 23, 1894 in Brighton, Illinois. (Her obituary was written by Philip Hehner who pastored Lake Creek 1859-61.) It appears that she may have had rheumatic fever. Reverend Fotsch was pastor at Lake Creek from 1875-1877.

JOHN C. MEYER

John C. Meyer was born September 21, 1831 in Niederberbecksen by the Rehme, Westfalen (Germany), and came with his parents in 1841 to Warren County, Missouri. His parents were among the first members of the Methodist Church which was founded by the Pioneer Preacher John Swahlen and Franz Horstmann. Under Brother Horstmann's influence, Brother Meyer was converted.

On May 31, 1853 in St. Louis, he married Karoline Blomberg. She was born January 11, 1831 in Sternberg, Lippe-Detmold, Germany.

During the dark years of the war, he was brought into the service. He lived in St. Louis where Brother Philipp Kuhl asked him to become a preacher. In 1865, he was sent out, and in 1866, he was accepted in the Southwest Missouri Conference.

**John C. Meyer
1877-1880.**

He served in the following communities: Second Creek, Missouri, 1865-68; Union including Beaufort, (now Leslie), 1868-71; Hopewell, 1871-74; Berger, 1874-77; Lake Creek, 1877-80; Concordia, 1880-82; Weston, Missouri and Fairmont, Kansas, 1883-84. In 1884-86, his name was added to the list of Superannuated preachers; he then lived in Corder, Missouri. He served thereafter in Lexington and Napoleon, Missouri in 1886; Atchison, Kansas, 1889-90. In 1890, he was superannuated and lived in Lexington, Missouri. Brother Meyer was an exacting and diligent worker and was well respected by his community. His record in the *Souvenir* indicated that he was a member of the Southwest Conference in 1866 and the West German Conference in 1879.

Karoline Meyer died March 11, 1903 and was buried at Lexington, Missouri beside their daughter Pauline.

JOHN HAUSAM, JR.

John Hausam, Jr. was born November 10, 1846 in Lee County, Iowa. He came to St. Charles County, Missouri as a young man, along with his parents, where he spent his youth. At the age of thirteen, he was converted under the influence of Reverend John G. Kost and joined the church. He was educated in the college at St. Charles and prepared himself for the ministry at Warrenton, Missouri. In 1868, he was admitted as a trial member of the Southwest Missouri Conference. In 1871 in St. Charles, Missouri, he married Elizabeth Frech. Their marriage was blessed with ten children.

In 1868, Reverend Hausam was ordained a minister of the Gospel at St. Charles in the German Methodist Episcopal Church. In 1879, he became a member of the West German Conference. His first charge was in Nebraska City, Nebraska in 1868; Pinckneyville, Illinois, 1869; Morrison and Chamois, 1870; for two years, he was inactive; Topeka, Kansas, 1873; Concordia, Missouri, 1874-77; Brunswick (now Dalton), 1877-80; Lake Creek, 1880-83; Cameron and Cosby, 1883-86. In 1886, he became supernumerated and in 1889, became superannuated.

John Hausam, Jr.
1880-1883.

While at Lake Creek, several children were born to them: Harris Peter Hausam, born July 21, 1880, and Maria Katherine Hausam, born April 26, 1882.

In 1886, the family moved to Sedalia, Missouri where they resided continuously, loved and respected by all who knew them. After retiring from the ministry, Reverend Hausam was engaged for a time in merchandising. In his last years, he traveled for the Mutual Assistance Company and made many friends in this position. He served God whenever there was an occasion. He was a healthy preacher and a faithful soul server who worked in many different communities with much success. In politics, he was a Republican and was once the nominee of his party for county treasurer, but was not elected.

He suffered many years with Bright's Disease; however, he was only ill for ten days. He died August 3, 1904, in his home at 1905 South Ingram Avenue, Sedalia, Missouri.

DANIEL WALTER

Daniel Walter was born November 11, 1833 at Lohningen, Kanton Schaffhausen, Switzerland. His Mother died when he was six, and his youth was marked with much hardship so that he seldom went to school and earned his keep among strange people until he was thirteen. In 1849, he emigrated to America and arrived poor and as a stranger in Chicago.

Under Reverend August Kellner, he was converted on Good Friday in 1852 and joined the Van Buren Street Congregation in Chicago. He responded to the call to the ministry, however, the lack of education kept him from the ministry for twenty years. In the Spring of 1874, he joined the Omaha Mission as a Presiding Elder. He worked 3-1/2 years and built two churches and a parsonage. His wife died and left him with four young children to raise.

He served in Lawrence, Kansas, 1877-79; Eudora, 1879-81, where he built a church; on account of delicate health, he took a supernumerated position for two years and then worked at Lake Creek, Missouri, 1883-86; Junction City, Kansas, 1886-87; as Administrator of the Central Wesleyan College, 1887-92, and took a superannuated status in 1894 and settled in Eudora Kansas.

Daniel Walter
1883-1886.

J. H. DREYER

J. H. Dreyer was born July 5, 1857 in St. Joseph, Missouri, the youngest son of Reverend Heinrich C. Dreyer, member of the Southwest German Conference, who served Lake Creek in 1848-49, and his wife Elisabeth Barbara Steininger.

In 1879, he attended Central Wesleyan College and graduated in 1882. In the Fall of the same year, he was accepted on trial in the West German Conference, and two years later, he attained full connection.

He married on September 28, 1882, Maria L. Steinley, daughter of Reverend Konstantin Steinley, and had seven children.

He served in the following communities: Great Bend, Kansas, 1882-84; Salina, 1884-86; Lake Creek, Missouri, 1886-88; Higginsville and Corder, 1888-92, during which time the church at Higginsville was built.

On account of increasing deafness in 1892, he was supernumerated, and 1898, became superannuated.

J. H. Dreyer
1886-1888.

HERMAN KOEPSEL

Herman Koepsel, born January 9, 1838 in Gorke Pommern, Germany, came with his parents, John and Sophia Koepsel, to America in the year 1848 and settled in Milwaukee, Wisconsin, then moved in 1849 to Manitowac.

Since they had no German Church in Manitowac, his parents sent him to Milwaukee where he was confirmed in a Lutheran Church. Through the efforts of Reverend Heinrich Wiethorn, he joined the Methodist Church on March 13, 1857. He received an exhorter's license from Reverend John Salzer in 1859.

On July 20, 1862, he married Fraulein Augustine Borchardt, daughter of Fredrich and Louise Borchardt, in Newton, Wisconsin.

He was a Private during the Civil War, Company C, 17th Regiment of Wisconsin, and served under General Sherman on his march from "Atlanta to the Sea." He came home weak, but was without wounds.

Herman Koepsel 1888-1891.

In 1866, he moved to Arago, Nebraska, and since they had no Methodist Church there, he and his family joined an Evangelical Community. In March, 1870, he was sent by the Kansas Conference of the Evangelical Community as preacher to Hamburg, Iowa, where he worked for two years. In 1872, he became a Deacon and in 1874, was ordained an Elder. He spent a year in Bloomington, Missouri; then three years at Platt River; two years at Holton, Kansas; Warrenburg and Clinton, four years; Yates Center, Kansas, three years; Newton, Kansas, one year; Wilson, one year. He left the Evangelical Community in 1887 and came back to the Methodist Church, serving in the following areas: Armourdale, Kansas; Lake Creek, Missouri, 1888-91; Eudora, Kansas, Salina, Fairmont, Parsons, and was with Reverend T. J. Brink and Friedrich Kaltenbach at Indiana Avenue and Southwest Boulevard, and with Jacob Tanner in Independence and Armourdale. In 1902, his name was on the list of superannuated preachers. He lived at that time in Kansas City, Kansas in a nice home. He enjoyed the evening of his life with God.

Several children were born to the Koepsels before coming to Lake Creek: Louis H., born October 7, 1864 in Wisconsin; Ida M., born July 24, 1866 in Nebraska; Minnie E., born August 11, 1868 in Nebraska; Rose A., born February 26, 1873 in Missouri; Anna B., born February 22, 1877 in Kansas; and Arthur E., born July 30, 1893 in Kansas. Two other daughters and a son, a Missionary in India, died before 1912.

The Koepsels left Kansas City, Missouri in 1907 and moved to Santa Ana, California. From Reverend Koepsel's Civil War pension papers, it was learned that he died November 25, 1913. The last paper in the file shows that his widow, Augustine Koepsel, died November 10, 1919.

HENRY H. HACKMAN

Henry H. Hackman was born at Hopewell, Warren County, Missouri May 23, 1855, where he grew to young manhood.

His parents who were members of the Evangelical Church gave him a religious upbringing. In 1875, he entered the Central Wesleyan College at Warrenton, Missouri, where he spent two years preparing himself for the teaching profession. During this time, he was converted under the pastorate of Charles Heidel and joined the church.

He felt the call to the Christian ministry. From 1879-1880, he was an instructor in an English and German Day School. In 1880, he received an exhorter's license through Reverend Charles Heidel and a preaching license through Reverend J. M. Dewein. About this time, he joined the West German Conference.

Henry H. Hackman
1891-1896.

On August 4, 1881 in New Melle, St. Charles County, Missouri, he was united in marriage to Miss Mina F. Riske, who died in July, 1922. Seven children, four sons and three daughters, were born to this marriage. In 1924, he married Fredrica Gassman.

The pastorates in which he ministered with visible success were Salina, Kansas, 1882-84; Great Bend, 1884-87. Here he had seven preaching places in four counties. He held splendid revivals and aided in erecting three churches: Larned, Kansas, 1887-88; Halstead and Newton, 1888-89, and Concordia, Missouri, 1889-91; he also preached at Alma and Waverly in 1891 and a church was built; Lake Creek, where campmeetings have been held since its founding, 1891-96; Swanton and Western, Nebraska, 1896-99; Sterling, 1899-1901; Waco and Seward, 1901; Eustis, 1906; Columbus, 1909; LaCrosse, Kansas, 1912; Otis, Kansas, 1913; Harvard, Nebraska, 1914; Columbus, 1916; Culbertson, 1924. He retired in 1926.

He was a faithful pastor. He had the spirit of awe and wondered at the beauty of God's word and His providence. He was always ready to give God due praise for His wonderful goodness. He was interested in education. All of his children attended Central Wesleyan College. One son was a minister, a member of the St. Louis Conference, and four were in the teaching profession.

After his retirement, he lived at Seward, Nebraska. He passed away at Lincoln, Nebraska on May 31, 1930. Interment was in Wyuka Cemetery.

F. H. WIPPERMANN

F. H. Wippermann was born September 24, 1861 at Pinckney, Warren County, Missouri. The fact that his parents were converted in 1870 and joined the Methodist Church made a lasting impression on the young boy. When he was fourteen, he was one of a class of ten who were tested by Reverend H. Bosholl in catechism and united with the church. On March 26, 1878, he received, after a long struggle, a sign of acceptance by God. The call to the ministry which he felt before his conversion was even more evident, and in the Fall of 1881, he attended Central Wesleyan College to prepare himself for the ministry.

In June, 1884, he was assigned to Custer, Nebraska. This was a new settlement which had many Germans who were not leaning toward the Methodist church or any other and only some, mostly Catholic families, could be encouraged to attend Sunday School and church. A few more were converted and joined the church.

F. H. Wippermann
1896-1900.

In September, 1884, he was accepted on trial. In 1885, he was sent from Custer to Stuart and Scottville, Nebraska. The District consisted of seven congregations and had a circumference of 180 miles. The annual salary was $185. In 1886, he was fully accepted into the Conference and ordained a Deacon.

On September 15, 1887, he married Matilde Thee at Rushville, Nebraska. He worked in Rushville and in the year 1888, was ordained an Elder. From 1889 to 1891, he served the Grand Island District.

The Palmer Church had a wonderful increase at a special assembly; a number of souls were converted to God, and twenty-two members who belonged to the Evangelical Community decided to join. He served at Humboldt, Nebraska, 1891-93 and Boonville, Missouri, 1893-96. The last years of his work were the best. From here, he went to Lake Creek District where, from 1896-1900, he was successfully active. From 1900-1903, he served the First Community in Kansas City, Kansas, which hosted the West German Conference in 1902 for the fifth time.

In the year 1903, Brother and Sister Wippermann were chosen as Administrators of the Orphans Home in Warrenton, Missouri.

The Wippermanns as Administrators at the Orphans Home in Warrentown, Missouri. 1904-1920

The February 8, 1945 issue of the *Kansas City Star* indicates that Reverend Wippermann, 83, had died February 6, 1945, at 34 South 32nd Street. Burial was at Warrenton, Missouri, his birthplace.

HENRY EDWARD ROMPEL

Henry Edward Rompel, familiarly known to his many friends and parishioners as "Dad" Rompel, was born in Louisville, Kentucky on April 10, 1871.

On September 19, 1895, he married Catharina Rebecca Demand, who was born March 2, 1869, seventh of nine children born to Heinrich and Margaretha Wahlers-Demand. She had brothers and sisters named Johann D. (a Methodist Episcopal pastor), Herman D., Martha Dorede Timken, Maria Katharina Sloan, George Heinrich, Carolina Louise Smith (married David Washington Smith, a Methodist Episcopal minister), Emelia Margaretha and Emma Rosina Demand. She grew up in a Christian family and was dedicated to the Lord at the Campmeeting in 1882 and subsequently joined the church. From 1890-92, she visited the children's home at Warrenton and then taught school in her hometown for two years.

After her marriage to Henry E. Rompel, she assisted him at their various appointments. With her retiring and undemanding manner, she quickly won the hearts of others and was an excellent influence. She dutifully carried out the responsibility of a preacher's wife and attended her doings by house visitations, conducting children's assemblies and the playing of the organ.

Henry Edward Rompel
1900-1901.

Henry Rompel was received on trial in the West German Conference of the Methodist Church in 1895 and into full membership in 1897. He served several pastorates in that Conference and for three years was a professor at Central Wesleyan College. In 1906, he was in school, and from that time on, he served charges in the Rock River (Illinois) Conference as follows: Norwood Park, Douglas Park and Centenary Church (Chicago), Bleeder, Waukegan, Ottawa Street (Joliet), Morris, First Church (Aurora), Grace Church (Elgin), Sheridan Road (Chicago), First and Epworth Churches (Ottawa), Community, McKinley Park and Lamon Avenue (Chicago). He pastored Lake Creek in 1900-1901.

He held degrees from the following institutions: Central Wesleyan College, B. S., 1901; D. D., 1916; Fenton Norman College, Ph. B., 1902; and Oskaloosa College, Ph. D., 1918.

Catharina endured surgery to remove a tumor and did not recover from the surgery. She died two week later on December 18, 1903. Shortly before her death, she was asked whether Jesus was with her, to which she replied, "Yes. I have put everything in order before I took this step."

On December 1, 1904, Henry Rompel remarried to Dorothea A. Albertson, who was born September 21, 1874 in Pekin, Illinois, the daughter of U. J. and Sophia Koch-Albertsen. She was a graduate of Bethseda Training School in Cincinnati and served as a deaconess in the Methodist Church until her marriage.

During the First World War while serving the church in Waukegan and later on special appointment, Reverend Rompel served as special chaplain at the Great Lakes Naval Training Station. It was during that time he received the name "Dad" by which he is known by a great number of people in many walks of life.

In addition to his many years in the preaching ministry, "Dad" Rompel was very active in various civic and character-building organizations. He was especially devoted to Boy Scout work and was a registered scouter from the time of the founding of the Boy Scouts of America in 1910, and was himself an Eagle Scout. He was the recipient of the highest award in Scouting on the regional basis, namely, the Silver Antelope award, as well as the Silver Beaver award. In the Methodist Church of Belvidere, a Scout room was dedicated to his memory, where he organized Scouting in 1912. He was also a past District Governor of Rotary International, 40th District, in 1923-24 and a 32° Mason.

Reverend Rompel retired in 1943 but continued as a supply pastor at Orland Park for Eight more years. In 1952, they moved to Morris, Illinois where they lived until December, 1955, at which time they became residents of the Methodist Old People's Home in Chicago. He died January 29, 1956 and was interred at Pekin, Illinois.

ERNST CREPIN

Ernst Crepin was born in March, 1865 in Berlin, Germany (where his father was an Inspection Assistant for the King).

He received a fine education in several schools in his hometown, and when he was fifteen years old, he was converted in the Lutheran Church. In 1884, through the work of the Order of Johanniter, he felt the call of the ministry but lost it again due to the nonchalant life he led.

In the year 1889, after some study of the English language, he came to the United States. In 1891, he took the first step in New York City toward becoming a United States Citizen. He completed the process in Sedalia, Missouri in 1903.

He came to America as thousands of Europeans and Asiatics before and after him had come to help build a new world and to build his own fortune. In the latter, he succeeded better than he had planned. He found the "Pearl of Great Price" in Wichita, Kansas where he went in 1891. He had previously united with the Methodist Church in 1890. He attended a business and trade school in Wichita, Kansas and again felt the call of the ministry.

In preparation for the ministry, he attended Central Wesleyan College in 1892-93. During the next four years, he completed the required course of study.

In 1891 in Wichita, Kansas, Reverend J. Haller encouraged him toward his goal. The Wichita Quarterly Conference in 1892 gave him an exhorter's license and in 1893, he received a local preacher's license and was recommended for membership in the West German Conference.

The West German Conference accepted him on trial, and in 1895, he became a Deacon. In 1897, he was ordained an Elder. He worked in the following locations: Guthrie and Orland, Oklahoma, 1893-94; Bison, Kansas, assistant, 1894-95; El Reno, Oklahoma, 1895-96; Norwich, Kansas, 1896-99; Arley and Liberty, Missouri, 1899-1901; Lake Creek, 1901-05; Lawrence, Kansas, 1905; supernumerated, 1906-08; Kramer, Nebraska, 1908-11; Wathena, Kansas, 1911-16; Lexington, Missouri, 1916-23; Lake Creek, 1923-27; Bland, Missouri, 1927-30. He retired in 1930

Ernst Crepin
1901-1905,
1923-1927.

In 1896, Ernst Crepin married Katie Buthman. To this union, five children were born. When his wife became an invalid in 1941, he had to retire completely, and they then made their home with their children. Katie Crepin died in March, 1946, and Ernst Crepin died at the home of his daughter, Arlene Miltenberger in Overland, Missouri on April 18, 1947.

GOTTLOB J. JAISER

Gottlob J. Jaiser was born February 13, 1857 in Kornwestheim, Wurttemberg, Germany. His parents were Jacob and Katharina Knoll-Jaiser. His parents were religious and tried to raise their children according to the Master.

Already in the early years, the spirit of God was in his heart, and he enjoyed to hear the words of God. He often expressed the wish as a boy of becoming a missionary. The minister who gave him his religious instruction recognized this wish and advised his father to let him study, but the father said that Gottlob was to be his successor, a blacksmith.

When he reached military age in 1877, he was drafted to the Cavalry, and in 1879, he became a student in the Veterinary School in Berlin and graduated with distinction.

He returned to the Regiment and was promoted to 2nd Lieutenant and was offered the opportunity to make it a career. He, however, did not enjoy the military life and returned home after completing his service time.

He now followed his father's wishes to become his successor, but the Master led him elsewhere.

In 1882, he emigrated to America. He arrived on March 4, 1882 in New York, going from there to St. Louis where he became acquainted with the German Methodist Church. It was there, under the leadership of Reverend C. Holtkamp in the Wash Street Church, that he was awakened to religion, and on July 16 of the same year, he went to York County, Nebraska. At a campmeeting at Kramer, Nebraska, he again felt the urge to become a preacher. In the Fall of 1882, he came to Warrenton to attend school. Dr. Kessler and Professor Rinckel accepted him, and Professor Sauer became his dear friend. In 1885, he finished his theology studies and joined the West German Conference.

He served the following charges: Oxford and Macon, Nebraska, 1885-88; Culbertson, 1888-89; in the State of California 1889-1894; Culbertson, Nebraska, 1894-95; Atchison, Kansas, 1895-97; Topeka, 1897-1902; Junction City, 1902-05; Lake Creek, Missouri, 1905-09.

Gottlob J. Jaiser
1905-1909.

On August 27, 1885, he married Emilie C. Nahrung of Osceola, Nebraska. There was no lack of suffering and sadness, but they sought their service for the Master to be the most rewarding that a being could give the Lord. In the future is their solution: In the Lord, through the Lord, with the Lord, and for the Lord.

GUSTAV F. MEYER

Gustav F. Meyer, son of John H. and Charlotte Meyer, was born near New Haven, Missouri on November 19, 1858. He hailed from a family of hardy pioneers who settled in Franklin County, Missouri in the early forties. His father was a charter member of the first German Methodist Church in the county, then known as "Meyer's Church."

Reared in the midst of such surroundings, he was confirmed in the Christian faith during the ministry of Reverend Charles Ott. Experiencing a "strange warming" of the heart during a series of evangelistic meetings, he felt the call to the Christian ministry.

He attended Wesleyan College whereupon, in 1887, he was assigned to Golden City, Missouri for his first appointment. With the exception of seven years which were spent in business, the years that followed were given to the ministry of the

Gustav F. Meyer
1909-1913.

following charges: Big Springs and Bland, Missouri of the St. Louis German Conference; Dalton, Missouri; Lake Creek, 1909-13; Russell and Alexander, Kansas of the West German Conference.

At his first charge, he became acquainted with Mary Habersaat, to whom he was married on July 9, 1887.

Reverend Meyer was a preacher of more than ordinary ability. He combined in himself an intensive knowledge of the Bible with a natural eloquence. His sermons were carefully thought out, systematic, and delivered with telling effect.

In 1920, he retired from the ministry, locating at Bazine, Kansas. In 1925, they moved to Junction City, Kansas where their daughters were employed as teachers and by whom they were lovingly cared for in their declining years. He died in 1948.

Rev. and Mrs. G. F. Meyer
1909-1913.

WALTER C. WAGNER

Walter C. Wagner was born October 5, 1883 at Avoka, Nebraska. His childhood days were spent at Burr, Nebraska, where his mother died when he was ten years old. He was one of six children.

He was converted at the age of sixteen years under the pastorate of Reverend J. J. Steininger. He felt the call of the ministry early but hesitated until he was nearly twenty-three.

During his early manhood, he was engaged in agricultural employment. His desire for the ministry took him to Central Wesleyan College at Warrenton, Missouri where he took a six-year course and graduated in June, 1913. He was a model student and did in reality eight years of work in the six years at Warrenton.

As a student, he served the Moberly church one year and the Herman church six months. He entered the West German Conference in September, 1913 and had charge of the Lake Creek and Florence churches four years.

Walter C. Wagner
1913-1917.

Soon after entering the West Conference, he married on November 27, 1913 Miss Gertrude Bohling, with whom he became acquainted in college. Three children were born to them.

From Lake Creek, his religious work took him to White Cloud, Kansas where he spent three years, and then to Enterprise, Kansas. Here, his health gave way, and he gave up the charge and rested six months at Paoli, Colorado. Then he went to

Harvard, Nebraska where he preached his last sermon Christian Sunday, sitting in a chair, his theme being "The Holy City," which he also sang.

Reverend Wagner died January 10, 1922 at Bethany Hospital. Funeral Services were held at the Eighth Street Methodist Episcopal Church, Kansas City on January 13 and at the Stover Methodist Episcopal Church on January 14, 1922. Many Lake Creek friends attended the service.

OSCAR F. KETTELKAMP

Oscar F. Kettelkamp was born December 30, 1890 in Nokomis, Illinois, the son of John W. and Ester Schneider-Kettelkamp. He had two brothers and a sister named Andrew B., Enoch G., Ben H., and Freda M. Meyers and two brothers who died in infancy.

Oscar Kettelkamp was converted in his youth. He received his religious training at the South Fork Methodist Church and was educated at Central Wesleyan College in Warrenton, Missouri. He was ordained in 1921 and was a member of the St. Louis Conference and the Missouri Conference during his years in the ministry.

On August 14, 1917, he married Elsie L. Bebermeyer. To them were born Aileen M. Myers and Olin F. Kettelkamp.

Reverend Kettelkamp served Lake Creek from 1917-1921. He retired from the ministry in 1958 and moved to Warrenton, Missouri where he died on October 9, 1961.

A. B. SCHOWENGERDT

A. B. Schowengerdt, son of Martin and Rosa Schowengerdt, was born at Berger, Missouri on August 6, 1879. At the age of nine, he and his family moved from Berger to a farm at Higginsville where he was reared. He attended rural grade school and the Higginsville High School. In 1901, he went to Kansas City to attend Business College for two years. At the completion of his business training, he secured a position with the George B. Peck Dry Goods Company as a bookkeeper and later as assistant cashier. He held this position for eighteen years.

In 1904, he married Mathilda E. Klee of Kansas City. To this union, five children were born, two sons preceding them in death. The remaining children are Mrs. G. W. Weheman, Mrs. J. H. Manthey, Jr. and A. B. Schowengerdt, Jr.

A. B. Schowengerdt
1921-1923
L. to R.: Rev. Schowengerdt, Stanley Rages, Paul Willis, Anna Rages, Vivian Demand, Phyllis Schowengerdt, Glenora Cole, Louella Ditzfeld.

Mr. Schowengerdt entered the ministry in October, 1921 when, at the conclusion of the annual conference in Kansas City, Lake Creek was left to be supplied, perhaps the only time ever. H. A. Hohenwald, District Superintendent, met with the quarterly conference, and it was decided to invite A. B. Schowengerdt to become the pastor at Lake Creek. He left his business and came. He was a sincere person, possessed a good character, and was well-liked by the congregation. While he pastored Lake Creek, a Woman's Society was organized (1923) and given the name "Helping Hand Society" with a charter membership of 37.

Reverend Schowengerdt was admitted into the Conference on September 3, 1922 and was ordained a Deacon on September 13, 1925 and an Elder on October 3, 1927.

During his twenty-seven years of ministry, he served the following churches in Missouri: Lake Creek, 1921-23; Lexington and Napoleon; El Dorado; Hume (Circuit); Willow Springs and Belle, where he was serving when he died August 20, 1948.

CHRISTIAN FERDINAND MAYER

Christian Ferdinand Mayer was born in Huntington, Indiana on March 21, 1876.

He began his ministry in 1896. During that first year, he married Meta Schumm, who died in 1928. To this marriage were born four sons, Andrew J., Edward C., Herbert and Michael.

Reverend Mayer attended the Methodist Blinn Memorial College at Brenham, Texas. After college, he was ordained and began his ministry on horseback and buggy. He endured many hardships of hunger and weather conditions while organizing small groups of people, mostly of German extraction. These groups of people became congregations.

His first real pastorate was in the city of Temple, Texas. Then he took the pastorate at Abilene, Texas, a wild and godless town. He served churches in Temple, McDaniels, Henrietta and Wichita Falls, Texas, and many country charges which had no names. While at Wichita Falls, Texas, he built the church and increased the membership. Then he moved to the north, serving churches in Madison, South Dakota; Waseca, Minnesota; and New Ulm, Minnesota. Back to Oklahoma, he served the church at the town of Waukomis, Oklahoma for four years. Then he went to Emporia, Kansas and then later moved to Moundridge, Kansas. This was his last charge in the Evangelical Association Church.

Reverend Christian F. Mayer (1927-1929) with confirmands Henry Demand, Lewis Hall, Ruth E. Gieschen, Hazel Hall and Bernice Hoehns.

From Moundridge, Kansas, he transferred to the Methodist Church, serving the Eighth Street Methodist Church in Kansas City, Kansas. He went to Oklahoma City, Oklahoma, then to Lake Creek near Smithton, Missouri, 1927-29. He served churches in Green Ridge and Aurora, Missouri. While at Lake Creek, he married Gesina Dorothy Schroder on May 16, 1928. While in Kansas, he served churches at LaCrosse, Kanopolis, McCracken, LaCygne, Lebo, Williamsburg and Mt. Zion.

Reverend Mayer's records show that he moved twenty-eight times in his forty-eight years of ministry. He was known as the big, moving preacher. He retired in 1944 and died July 18, 1948 at Baldwin City, Kansas.

MAX OPP

Max Opp was born February 7, 1879 in Germany and was brought by his parents to America when he was four years of age.

In 1908, he married Ida Revoir of Doe Run, Missouri. Into this Christian home were born Eleanor Opp-Robinson and Armel Opp.

After graduation from Central Wesleyan College at Warrenton, Missouri, he was ordained into the Christian ministry and became a member of the Methodist Conference in 1908. The following charges were served: Copenhagen, Missouri; Burton, Illinois; Nokomis, Illinois; Leslie, Missouri; St. Louis (Zion),Missouri; Ellis Grove, Illinois; Perryville, Missouri; Smithton (Lake Creek), 1929-36; Gordonville, Missouri; Concordia, Missouri; Sedalia Circuit, Missouri; Bronaugh, Missouri; Drake, Missouri; Berger, Missouri; Belle, Missouri; and St. James, Missouri.

Max Opp
1929-1936.

It was most natural for the Reverend Opp to witness in season and out of season for His Lord and God's love. Be he shopkeeper or professional man, he gave his testimony in word and deed of the Spirit within one, when Jesus comes into the heart.

Wherever the parsonage was, the temporary living place of the family, flowers were a hallmark of his hobby, specializing in the common garden varieties. He took time out, never too busy to listen. His pastoral calling was a favorite aspect of this vocation, and he delighted in home visitation.

At his retirement in 1953, Reverend and Mrs. Opp moved to Salt Lake City, Utah to live near his daughter and her family. He died April 22, 1965. Funeral services were held at Memorial Methodist Church in Farmington, Missouri, and interment was in the Parkview Cemetery there.

RAY MASSEY BROWN

Ray Massey Brown was born in Jeffersonville, Illinois on September 4, 1878. His background was Methodist and Christian. His maternal grandfather, James M. Massey, was a charter member of the Southern Illinois Conference. Two uncles R. H. Massey and T. J. Massey were members of the Conference at a later date.

His childhood home was Christian where he heard God's Word read and the voices of his parents lifted in prayer. His acceptance of Christ as his personal Savior at the age of eleven was a definite experience.

On June 15, 1903, he married Mary Finely of Wayne County, Illinois. She, too, was of Christian Methodist parentage and journeyed life's way as a faithful companion and contributed her full share to her husband's ministry. Three children brightened and blessed their parsonage home; Virgil E., Harold B., and Neva.

His call to the ministry came in his young manhood. After teaching school for four years, he responded to the call and joined the Southern Illinois Conference. He served the following pastoral charges in Southern Illinois: Oblong Circuit, Wheeler, Calhoun, Sailor Springs, Norris City, Mason, Drossville and North Prairie; Webster, Randolph, Madison, Grenola, Hoyt and Burlingame in Kansas; Puxico, Tipton, Lake Creek, 1936-39; and Stockton in Missouri. In all, he completed a preaching and pastoral ministry of forty-three years.

Reverend Brown was an effective and evangelistic preacher, and people were led to Christ in every charge that he pastored. He inspired and led in three church building achievements. The missionary and benevolent enterprises of the church were near to his heart, and he helped all of his congregations to a Christian world outlook. (Reverend Ray M. Brown christened me at Grandpa Hoehns' on November 14, 1937!)

Ray Massey Brown 1936-1939.

Reverend Brown loved to work in the soil to plant, to cultivate and to harvest. Caring for a garden or truck patch was his favorite hobby.

A stroke on January 1, 1950 left him partially paralyzed and confined to bed. The main responsibility for his care was undertaken by his wife. His weary body succumbed to the strain, and his spirit was wafted to its God on the evening of October 20, 1950.

Reverend Brown's widow Mary spent her remaining years in the Methodist Home in Topeka, Kansas. She died in April, 1964 and was interred beside him near Geff, Illinois.

EDWARD LOUIS RATHERT

Edward Louis Rathert was born at Berger, Franklin County, Missouri on November 27, 1875, the son of Adolph Carl and Louise Laaker-Rathert. He was the fifth child, his brothers and sisters being C. G. William, Friedericke E. Stoeppelman, Christine Wolters and Louis Charles Rathert. His Mother died when he was an infant, and his father remarried. He had stepbrothers and stepsisters named Louise D. A. Weber, Ida A. Freitag, Emma P. Eisenmann, Louis O. S., Ottillie K. Kollmeyer, Paul A., Simon G., Elda A. Bade-Wade and Lydia V. Bryan.

His conversion occurred while he attended the Senate Grove Methodist Church. His early education was received in the Franklin County Schools. He attended Central Wesleyan College at Warrenton, graduating with the Class of 1905.

He entered the ministry through the St. Louis German Conference in September, 1905. He preached in this conference from 1905 to 1912 and from 1917 to 1926. He was ordained a Deacon on September 29, 1907 and an Elder on September 19, 1909. He was a member of and preached in the Missouri Conference from 1926 to 1935 and in the Southwest Missouri Conference from 1935 to 1957.

He was married at Senate Grove, Missouri on July 6, 1905 to Caroline Charlotte Wiemeyer. They were the parents of two daughters, Mayme Charlotte Rathert-Blinne and Esther Lena Rathert-Page.

On March 6, 1921, Reverend Rathert remarried at Anaheim, California to Dorothea Caroline Katharina Tuschoff, the daughter of Charles and Minnie Tuschoff. She was born at Old Appleton, Missouri on March 12, 1883. As a young woman, she was active in the Zion Methodist Church at Old Appleton, taking part in the choir, Sunday School and Women's Society. She died November 12, 1959.

Reverend Rathert was pastor at Lake Creek when they celebrated one hundred years of existence in 1943. He prepared the booklet with the blue cover that has now become so scarce. He retired in 1948 from active ministry though he continued for several years to preach. In all, he preached forty-seven years at the following charges: Waltersburg, Illinois; Bible Grove; Bushnell; Rayville; Metropolis, Illinois; Old Appleton, Missouri; Jamestown; Etna; Greencastle; Osborn; Coffey; Leslie; Lake Creek, 1939-49; and Pleasant Green, Missouri.

Reverend Rathert died at the Fairview Nursing Home on September 10, 1967 where he resided for some time. He and his wife Dorothea were both buried in the Smithton Cemetery.

Edward Louis Rathert 1939-1949.

Rev. Stribling, Rev. Wasson, Rev. Rathert, Rev. Dillon, Rev. Burton.

HERSCHEL BENTON FLY

Herschel Benton Fly was born near Verona, Missouri on August 28, 1893, the son of Reverend and Mrs. C. A. Fly.

He made his home in the community of his birth with the exception of six years that he lived near Sedalia and Clinton, Missouri.

On August 14, 1924, he was married to Hila Stockton. To this union were born three children: Imogene, Eugene and Thomas Fly.

He pastored churches in Washburn, Bethlehem, Onward and Pharr's Springs, all in southwest Missouri. He also pastored Lake Creek, 1949-51; Calhoun, Drake's Chapel, Deepwater and Lowry City, in the Sedalia District.

He died May 31, 1963 and was interred in the Calton Cemetery near Monett.

Herschel Benton Fly
1949-1951.

REUBEN E. OLIN

Reuben E. Olin was born September 30, 1899. He married Dorothy Pontius, daughter of Allen G. and Grace Pontius. Dorothy was born March 2, 1905 and died December 20, 1964 at Topeka, Kansas. After Dorothy's death, Reuben remarried.

Their surviving daughter, Laura Grace, was a marvelous singer. During their appointment at Lake Creek, Laura Grace sang a solo each Sunday and I accompanied her.

Reuben E. Olin served Lowry City preceding his appointment to Lake Creek. He was at Lake Creek in 1951 and 1952. From Lake Creek, he was assigned to Creighton, Missouri.

Reuben Olin died November 4, 1968 as the result of an automobile accident.

Reuben E. Olin
1951-1952.

JACOB COLESON PASCHAL

Jacob Coleson Paschal was born September 22, 1882 in Bedford County, Tennessee.

He was educated in the Tennessee schools, graduating from Tennessee Normal, and taught school for a time in Tennessee.

96 *Chapter V*

On July 31, 1904, he married Levina Ruth Keen, also a teacher. To this union were born six children: Paul C., Thomas A., Martha E. Ingram, Zilpha Elwell, Margaret Schnelle and J. C. Paschal. Levina Paschal died in 1945, and Jacob remarried on November 4, 1948 to Mary E. Hadley. Mary had children by her former marriage named India Jackson, Mrs. D. O. Caress and Mrs. George D. Thompson.

Jacob C. Paschal entered the Methodist ministry in 1914 in the Middle Tennessee Conference. He transferred to the Kansas Conference in 1932. He was a charter member of the Central Kansas Conference. He took a retired relationship in 1948 and supplied charges in Missouri until 1955 when he came back to Covert, Kansas. He lived in Dodge City the last years of his life.

Reverend Paschal was a member of several Masonic bodies and the Order of the Eastern Star. He died at Trinity Hospital in Dodge City, Kansas on September 3, 1958 and was interred in Walnut Hill Cemetery, Kingman, Kansas beside his first wife.

Jacob Coleson Paschal
1952-1955.

DONALD RUSSELL ESTES

Donald Russell Estes was born December 10, 1934, son of Floyd and Lela Fowler-Estes. He attended grade and high school in Polo and then attended Central Methodist College, receiving his B. A. degree in 1955. His theological training was at St. Paul School of Theology in Kansas City.

On August 28, 1954, he was married to Nina Rose Bitner. This union was blessed with three children: Andrew, Jeffrey and Steve.

In 1956, Russell was admitted to the Southwest Missouri Conference. He was ordained a Deacon in 1960 and an Elder in 1965. He served the following appointments: Braymer Circuit; Orrick; Lake Creek, 1955-57; Lincoln and Ionia; Wellington; Sumner and Rothville; Anderson; Goodman; Hopkins; Hale and Bosworth; and Drexel.

Russell died while serving at Drexel on July 11, 1974.

Donald Russell Estes
1955-1957.

LINUS EAKER

Linus Eaker was born August 29, 1886 at Zalma, Bollinger County, Missouri, one of four children born to Fred and Mary Gaines-Eaker. His siblings were Marvin, Glenn and Vena Eaker.

Under the influence of Reverend L. L. Pinnell, and the influence of his Christian parents, he was converted. In 1907, he was admitted on probation to the former St. Louis Conference. He took four years of correspondence courses through Southern Methodist University, Dallas, Texas, and studied continuously from books provided by Vanderbilt University, Nashville, Tennessee. He was ordained in 1918.

Reverend Eaker served pastorates at Doniphan, Williamsville, Bloomfield, Lutesville, Farmington Stations, Campbell, Bonne Terre, Desloge, Bloomfield, Rich Hill, Webb City, Troost Avenue in Kansas City, Slater, Neosho, Clinton, Lake Creek, 1957-70; and Pleasant Hill. He was District Superintendent of the Marshall District from 1951 to 1957.

**Linus Eaker
1957-1970.**

He retired in 1957 with a service record of nearly fifty years, more that any other pastor in the West Conference, and one of the longest in United Methodism. His last pastorate was at the Lake Creek and Pleasant Hill churches near Sedalia where he served thirteen years after his retirement.

Reverend Eaker died October 12, 1977 at the Brooking Park Geriatric Center. Funeral services were held October 14, 1977 with the Reverend Hubert Neth and Reverend James R. McQueen officiating. Burial was in Highland Sacred Gardens, Sedalia.

JERRY M. MOON

Jerry Max Moon was born October 25, 1930 in Webb City, Jasper County, Missouri, son of Gradon D. and Mildred Ann Kent-Moon. His father was a meatcutter who was initially in business with his twin brother in Oklahoma; he later was in business in Springfield, Missouri. Jerry had one brother, Gradon A. Moon.

Jerry graduated from Springfield High School in 1949; he attended Central Methodist College, earning a double major in sociology and religious education and a minor in Psychology. He did special schooling at Southern Methodist University, Dallas, Texas and at St. Paul's and Perkins. He later took Advanced Administration at Scarrett College.

On August 7, 1955, he married Helen Joan Hammond. To them were born Cynthia Marie and Susan Maelene Moon.

Jerry's parents, along with a Sunday School teacher he had at Campbell Avenue Methodist Church in Springfield, were influential in his entrance into the ministry. From this particular church emerged seven pastors! While Jerry was in the Marine Corps (1949-53), he assisted a young Episcopal priest who served as Chaplain.

He was licensed to preach in 1953 and ordained an Elder in 1954. From 1953-63, he served pastorates in Fayette (circuit); Moberly (Trinity Associated); LaMonte; Grain Valley; and Ravenwood. From September, 1963 to September, 1968, he and Joan served as Executive Directors of the Dulac Community Center in Dulac, Louisiana. After a one-year Sabbatical in Raytown, they served in Smithton from 1969-1976. The first year, Florence was paired with Smithton, and then Lake Creek was paired with Smithton. His remaining appointments were St. James and Joplin, 1976-80; Jasper, 1980-82; Appleton City, 1982-87; Fairfax, 1987-89; and Milan, 1989-91. He took disability leave in 1991.

Jerry Max Moon
1970-1973.

JAMES R. MCQUEEN
(1973-78)

Jim McQueen entered probationary status in the Missouri West Conference in 1962 and a full connection in 1965. To date his appointments have been to Miller, 1951; Villa Heights, Joplin, 1956-64; Carl Junction, 1964-69; Mount Carmel, Springfield, 1969-70; Gallatin, 1970-73; Sedalia, Epworth and Lake Creek, 1973-78; Mountain Grove, 1978-90. He retired in 1990.

DWIGHT RAY BINGHAM

Dwight Ray Bingham was born December 5, 1914 in Dallas, Iowa, one of four sons born to Walter Samuel and Mabel Germane Hunter-Bingham. His brothers are named Eldon, Lloyd and Kenneth Bingham.

Though Dwight traveled a somewhat conventional road on his journey to become a minister (progressing through the local church, ordination as a deacon in another denomination, the offices of Sunday School superintendent and teacher, lay speaking), a Reverend Robert C. Waters was influential in his life. He pastors congregations who are much like he is . . . loyal members . . . while paying off parsonage and church building debts, enacting some construction programs, helping people who need help and, in turn, being helped by them.

Dwight, on August 30, 1936 in Paris, Missouri married Dorothy Lee Ashcraft. A son, Emmett Ray Bingham, was born to them. In Braymer, Missouri in May, 1956, he married Donna Faye Henkins-Evans. A son, Terry William Bingham, was born to them. On August 3, 1968 in Chillicothe, he married Dorothy Ida Kauffman-Reid. Both sons are now married and have families of their own.

Dwight pastored the Hallsville Circuit 1956-60 while procuring his B. A. degree from Central Methodist College. He was assigned to New Franklin and Clark's Chapel in 1960-63 while he procured his Bachelor of Divinity degree from Saint Paul's School of Theology. He was assigned to Milan Parish, 1963-68; Slater and Gilliam, 1968-78; Epworth and Lake Creek, 1978-85. He has been on the Conference Board of Ministries for eight years; was District Missionary coordinator for the Chillicothe District, and a board member on the District Council of Ministries for fourteen years.

**Dwight Ray Bingham
1978-1985.**

RICHARD A. SEATON

Richard Arnwine Seaton was born November 17, 1940 in Richmond, Ray County, Missouri, youngest son of Homer Tipton and Lena Lee Arnwine-Seaton. He had brothers and a sister named Virginia Ingle, Homer T. and James Bruce Seaton.

His father worked for Standard Oil, was a District Manager for Metropolitan Life Insurance for many years, and worked for the Post Office Department from 1948 until his retirement.

Richard graduated from Lexington High School in 1958, then attended C.M.S.C., graduating in 1965. Graduate work was at Saint Paul's School of Theology in Kansas City where he received a Bachelor of Divinity and Master of Divinity degrees. Doctoral work in Blue Collar Ministry was also done at Saint Paul's.

**Richard Arnwine Seaton
1985-1990.**

Richard's parents were also instrumental in his decision to enter the ministry, as were the messages in the printed sermons of John Wesley. Richard was part of a Bible study group and was converted while he was stationed in Germany. He was licensed to preach in 1962, ordained a deacon in 1966 and an elder in 1969.

In 1969, he was sent to Kansas City to integrate the Swope Park Methodist Church. In 1978, he was selected as Man of the Year in Kansas City by the Jackson County V.F.W. and by the City Council for Youth Services in 1978-79. Richard compiled and wrote the *History of the United Methodist Churches of Missouri* which was published in 1984. He was the first Chairperson of Archives and History from 1968-76; he was reappointed to the post again in 1980 and assisted in organizing the Missouri Methodist Historical Society and was their first president in 1983.

His appointments have been to Zion Hill (Lafayette County), 1964; Concordia was added to Zion Hill in 1965, and he had both charges until 1969; Swope Park, 1969-75; special appointment in Southeast Kansas City (served three months as interim pastor of Epworth and Roanoke Methodist Churches), 1975; White Avenue, 1976-82; Platte City, 1982-85; Epworth (Sedalia) and Lake Creek, 1985-90.

Richard retired from the itinerant ministry in 1990 and now serves the Leeton-Eldorado congregations in retirement. He is still busily involved in Methodist history!

BRENDA GOODRUM WEST

Brenda Goodrum West was born October 26, 1951 at Hayti, Pemiscot County, Missouri, one of two daughters born to Mack Inland and Ruby Lois Mangold-Goodrum. Her father was a farmer and her mother a housewife. Her sister Barbara Lipe is a hairstylist in Memphis, Tennessee.

Brenda graduated from Deering Elementary School (renamed Delta after consolidation). She earned a Bachelor of Arts degree in English Literature from Lambuth College in Jackson, Tennessee and a Minister of Divinity degree from Saint Paul's graduating in 1981.

**Brenda Goodrum West
1990-Present.**

She was encouraged in her career choice by her parents and her grandmother. She experienced several revelations while working with junior high youth after college graduation and while serving as the youth minister in Warrensburg.

On August 9, 1974 at the United Methodist Church in Hayti, Missouri, Brenda married James Edward West, a native of Dexter, Missouri. Jim is pastor of the United Methodist Church in Windsor where they reside, while Brenda is pastor of the Epworth (Sedalia) and Lake Creek circuit. They have one son, James Joseph West.

Brenda's charges thus far have been to Centennial Parish, Henry County, 1981-85; Carterville, 1985-87; Associate Pastor at First United Methodist Church, Carthage, 1987-89; campus minister at C.M.S.U., Warrensburg, 1989-90; Epworth (Sedalia) and Lake Creek, 1990 to the present.

Brenda has served as Registrar of the Board of Ordained Ministry for the annual conference; was a delegate to General Conference and Jurisdictional Conference in 1988; has been on conference Council on Ministries and is Chaplain for Bothwell Hospital Hospice.

BIBLIOGRAPHY FOR *THE OBEDIENT ONES*

Barth, Sebastian—*Indianapolis News*, August 27, 1904, p. 5; *Commemorative Biographical Record of Prominent and Representative Men of Indianapolis and Vicinity*, pp. 173-175; *Indianapolis News*, September 16, 1912, p. 12.

Bingham, Dwight R.—Information supplied by Dwight Bingham, January 4, 1993.

Brown, Ray M.—Obituary furnished by Dr. Virgil E. Brown, Sabetha, Kansas, June 11, 1967.

Crepin, Ernst—Obituary furnished by Loretta Ehmke, Independence, Missouri, September 26, 1966; *Souvenir der West Deutschen Konferenz der Bischoeflichen Methodistenkirche*, Kriege, Becker, Hermann, Koerner; Jennings & Graham, Cincinnati, Ohio, 1906, p. 279 (translated by Armin H. Ciersdorff).

Dreyer, Heinrich C.—Obituary published in *Minutes of Annual Southwest German Conference of the Methodist Episcopal Church, 1870*, p. 255; *The Story of German Methodism, The Biography of an Immigrant Soul*, Douglass, The Methodist Book Concern, Cincinnati, 1939, p. 56.

Dreyer, J. H.—*Souvenir*, p. 249 (translated by Armin H. Ciersdorff).

Eaker, Linus—Letter from Linus Eaker dated June 23, 1967; obituary, *Sedalia Democrat*, October 14, 1967.

Eisenmeyer, Konrad—*Souvenir*, pp. 13, 17.

Estes, D. Russell—Information from *Conference Journal*, 1974.

Feisel, Jacob—*Christliche Apologete*, July 30, 1902, entitled "Out of the Time of the Father, The Life and Works of the Preacher, Jacob Feisel" by J. Schlagenhaus (translated by Armin H. Ciersdorff).

Fly, Herschel B.—Memorial article furnished by Hila Fly, Monett, Missouri, April 14, 1967.

Fotsch, William—*Christliche Apologete*, Memorial, by H. H. Schweitert, DeSoto, Missouri (translated by Armin H. Ciersdorff).

Hackman, Henry H.—*Minutes of the 70th Session of Nebraska Annual Conference of the Methodist Episcopal Church*, Lincoln, Nebraska, September 16 to September 22, 1930, p. 635.

Hankemeyer, Heinrich—Memorial, Conference Minutes (Translated by Carol Rexroad, Columbia, Missouri); *Lake Creek Baptismal Records*, 1869.

Hausam, John J.—*Souvenir*, Memoire of John Hausam by Samuel Buechner, Sedalia, p. 236; obituary, *Sedalia Democrat*, August 5, 1904; *Souvenir*, pp. 29, 237; letter from Elizabeth Wilcoxson, Kansas City, Missouri dated October 12, 1966; *Lake Creek Baptismal Records, 1880, 1882*.

Hausam, John Sr.—*Souvenir*, pp. 20-21; *Lake Creek Baptismal Records*, 1851.

Hehner, Philip—*Christliche Apologete, 1909* (translated by Armin H. Ciersdorff); G.S.A. Civil War Pension Papers, file #92249.

Hellweg, Peter—*Christliche Apologete*, February 25, 1897, by Carl A. Schuldt, Garner, Iowa (translated by Armin H. Ciersdorff).

Hilmer, Leonhard G.—*Souvenir*, pp. 66, 82.

Holzbeierlein, Andrea—Letters from Edna G. Holzbeierlein dated February 28, 1969 and March 18, 1969; letter from Lydia Sleyster Lovestedt dated March 24, 1969; marriage record, Recorder's Office, Pettis County, Missouri, Book B, p. 60; obituary of Emma M. Holzbeierlein-Sleyster.

Jaiser, Gottlob J.—*Souvenir*, p. 303 (translated by Armin H. Ciersdorff).

Jacoby, L. S.—Minutes of Annual Conference of M. E. Church, 1874, p. 88.

Kettelkamp, Oscar F.—Letter from Ms. O. F. Kettelkamp dated April 20, 1967.

Koepsel, Herman—*Souvenir*, p. 256 (translated by Armin H. Ciersdorff); Golden Wedding article by C. F. Kuhnle of South Hollywood, California (translated by Armin H. Ciersdorff); G.S.A. Civil War Pension Papers, file #786807; death certificate, Orange County, #147.

Lahrmann, Heinrich—Obituary from *Journal, St. Louis German Conference*, 1891, pp. 82-84 (translated by Carol Rexroad, Columbia, Missouri).

Magly, Jacob—(translated by Armin H. Ciersdorff).

Mahnken, Herman—Newspaper obituary dated December, 1917.

Mayer, Christian F.—Material furnished by Edward C. Mayer, Sr. dated May 29, 1967.

McQueen, James R.—*Journal of the Missouri West Conference, Central District, 1988*.

Meyer, Gustav F.—Obituary furnished by Reverend Zwingli Meyer.

Meyer, John C.—*Souvenir*, p. 260 (translated by Armin H. Ciersdorff); obituary of Karoline Meyer dated March, 1903 (translated by Armin H. Ciersdorff).

Miller, John P.—Obituary from *St. Louis German Annual Conference Journal*, 1916, p. 38.

Moon, M. Jerry—Information furnished by Jerry and Joan Moon.

Niedermeier, William—*Souvenir*, pp. 19, 81.

Nuelsen, Heinrich—*Christliche Apologete*, August 30, 1911 (translated by Carol Rexroad, Columbia, Missouri).

Olin, Reuben E.—Information furnished by Esther Brown, Creighton, Missouri dated may 6, 1976; letter from Alfred E. Pontius, DeFuniak Springs, Florida, dated September 8, 1976.

Opp, Max—*Minutes of Missouri East Annual Conference, 1965*, pp. 174, 175; letter from Ms. Carl Opp, Sedalia, Missouri dated April 13, 1967; letter from Eleanor Opp-Robinson dated April 30, 1967.

Paschal, Jacob C.—Letter and obituary information from India L. Jackson dated November 4, 1967.

Rathert, Edward L.—Obituary of Caroline Rathert by C. A. Neumeyer, Cape Girardeau, Missouri (translated by Armin H. Ciersdorff); obituary of Dora Rathert from *Sedalia Democrat*, dated November, 1959; obituary of Edward L. Rathert from *Sedalia Democrat*, dated September 11, 1967; letter from Mayme Rathert-Blinne dated August 1, 1967.

Ringen, Conrad—Obituary from *Christliche Apologete* dated December, 1903; obituary of Margaretha Hoehns-Ringen dated 1896 (both translated by Armin H. Ciersdorff).

Rompel, Henry C.—Obituary of Katharina R. Rompel, 1903; *Minutes of Rock River Annual Conference, 1956*, pp. 249-250; obituary of Dorothea Albertsen-Rompel from *Minutes of Rock River Annual Conference, 1956*, pp. 254-255.

Schatz, J. George—Obituary from *Southwest German Conference Journal*, 1872, p. 81; *Lake Creek Baptismal Records*, 1867.

Schowengerdt, A. B.—Obituary from *Minutes of Annual Conference, St. Louis Conference, 1948*, p. 58.

Schreck, William—Obituary from *Minutes of Annual Conference of Methodist Episcopal Church, 1874*, p. 88.

Seaton, Richard A.—Information supplied by Richard A. Seaton.

Stueckemann, Charles H.—Obituary from *Minutes of Annual St. Louis German Conference of the Methodist Episcopal Church, 1883*, p. 317; *Lake Creek Baptismal Records, 1864.*

Wagner, Walter C.—Obituary from Stover newspaper; letter from Gertrude Wagner dated May 6, 1967.

Walter, Daniel—*Souvenir*, p. 267 (translated by Armin H. Ciersdorff).

West, Brenda G.—Information supplied by Brenda G. West.

Wippermann, F. H.—*Souvenir*, p. 350 (translated by Armin H. Ciersdorff); obituary from *Kansas City Star*, Wednesday, February 7, 1945.

Appendices
LIST OF PASTORS OF LAKE CREEK CHURCH

1839-40—Francis Walkenhorst-(Lay Pastor)
1843-45—Sebastian Barth
1844-45—Heinrich Nuelsen
1845-47—Conrad Eisenmeyer
1845-95—Herman Mahnken(Lay Preacher)
1847-48—Wilhelm Schreck
1848-49—Heinrich C. Dreher
1849-50—Jacob Feisel
1850-51—Wilhelm Neidermeier
1851-52—John Hausam, Sr.
1852-53—Jacob Feisel
1853-55—Peter Hellweg
1855-57—Heinrich Lahrmann
1857-59—Jacob Maegly
1859-61—Philip Hehner
1861-63—Civil War—No Pastor
1863-64—Andreas Holzbeierlein
1864-66—Charles Stuckemann
1866-69—George Schatz
1869-71—Heinrich Hankemeyer
1871-73—John Philip Miller
1873-75—Leonhard Gottfried Hilmer
1875-77—William Fotsch
1877-80—John C. Meyer
1880-83—John Hausam, Jr.
1883-86—Dan Walter
1886-88—J. H. Dreyer
1888-91—Herman Koepsel
1891-96—Henry H. Hackmann
1896-1900—F. H. Wipperman
1900-01—Henry Edward Rompel
1901-05—Ernst Crepin
1905-09—Gottleib J. Jaiser
1909-13—Gustav F. Meyer
1913-17—Walter Wagner
1917-21—Oscar F. Kettelkamp
1921-23—A. B. Schowengerdt
1923-27—Ernst Crepin
1927-29—Christian Ferdinand Mayer
1929-36—Max Opp
1936-39—Ray Massey Brown
1939-49—Edward Louis Rathert
1949-51—Herschel Benton Fly
1951-52—Reuben E. Olin
1952-55—Jacob Coleson Paschal
1955-57—Russell Estes
1957-70—Linus Eaker
1970-73—Jerry Moon
1973-78—James McQueen
1978-85—Dwight Bingham
1985-90—Richard Seaton
1990-Present—Brenda West

PRESIDING ELDERS OR DISTRICT SUPERINTENDENTS WHO SERVED LAKE CREEK FROM THE BEGINNING

Dr. Wilhelm Nast, the founder of German Methodism sent the first Missionary in 1843.

In 1844 the German Churches were organized into German speaking Districts and the St. Louis German District was formed.

1844-45—Dr. Ludwig Jacoby
1845-48—Heinrich Koeneke: Missouri District Organized
1848-50—Wilhelm Schreck
1850-52—Friederich Kerkman
1852-54—Philip Kuhl
1854-56—William Fiegembaum
1856-57—John Hausam
1857-62—Jacob Feisel: Due to the war the Kansas Conference appointed the next superintendent.
1862-64—Constantine Steinley

In 1864 the German Districts were organized into German Conferences. The Southwest German Conference was formed and Lake Creek was in the St. Louis District

1864-65—Philip Kuhl
1865-66—John G. Kost
1866-67—William Schnierle
1867-68—Fr. Stoffregen
1868-70—F. W. Meyer
1870-72—Henry Fiegenbaum
1872-74—Jacob Tanner
1874-75—William Schwind
1875-77—Jacob Tanner
1877-79—E. H. Kriege

In 1878 the Southwest Conference was divided into the St. Louis and the West German Conferences. Lake Creek was in the West German Conference and placed in the Kansas City District.

In 1879 it was placed in the St. Joseph District and in 1880 in the Missouri District.

1879-83—Henry Fiegenbaum
1883-85—H. R. Riemer
1885-89—J. G. Leist
1889-90—John H. Asling
1890-96—John Demand

In 1893 the district name was once again changed to the Kansas City District.

1896-1902—Charles Ott
1902-08—John H. Asling
1908-14—D. W. Smith
1914-22—H. A. Hohenwald
1922-26—D. W. Smith

In 1926 the German conferences were merged with the English conferences and Lake Creek was in the St. Louis Conference and Sedalia District.

1926-30—J. C. Gilbreth
1930-32—Wm. Riley Nelson

In 1931 the St. Louis Conference merged with the Missouri Conference.

1932-33—Harvey A. Jones
1933-39—A. A. Halter

In 1939 the three branches of Methodism United.

1939-41—L. M. Starkey, Sr.
1941-42—Freeman Havingherst
1942-48—A. H. Asling
1948-54—E. W. Bartley
1954-60—Robert M. Lehew
1960-62—Mark S. Horn
1962-68—Herbert Hillme
1968-71—N. Clinton Chasteen
1971-76—Edward A. Neimeyer
1976-81—Hubert Neth
1981-87—Marie Hyatt
1987-89—A. Fritz Mutti
1989—Champ Breeden

CONSTITUTION OF THE LAKE CREEK CAMP MEETING ASSOCIATION

Article I

The name of this organization shall be the Lake Creek Camp Meeting Association.

Article II

The aim and purpose of the organization shall be to promote evangelistic and educational interests of the community.

Article III
1. The officers of the organization shall be a President, Vice-President, Secretary and Treasurer and a Board of Directors as hereinafter provided.
2. The President, Vice-President, Secretary and Treasurer shall be elected at a meeting of the Board called by the President during the Camp Meeting Session.
3. The Board of Directors shall consist of at least nine members with at least two members from each of the participating congregations.

Article IV
1. The duties of the President shall be: To call all meetings of the Board and preside at these meetings. He shall have no vote except in case of a tie.
2. The Vice-President shall assist the President in his duties and act as chairman in case of his absence.
3. The Secretary shall keep an accurate record of the minutes of all meetings and of the membership of the organization.
4. The Treasurer shall receive and care for all funds and pay all orders as the Board may direct and keep an accurate account of all income and expenditures.
5. The Board of Directors shall meet at the campground at the call of the President not later than June 15 of each year:
    (1) To examine the association property and arrange for any repair work deemed necessary and beneficial.
    (2) To approve speakers for the worship services as suggested by the Pastor of the Lake Creek Church.
    (3) To appoint committees, such as Housing, Water & Sanitation, Lighting, Meat, Straw, Preacher's Tent and any others that shall be deemed necessary.
    (4) To advise with the President regarding the workers necessary for the success of the Camp Meeting and to suggest any choice of their respective congregations.
    (5) The Board shall maintain insurance on all association property sufficient to cover any loss which may be sustained.

Article V

Any congregation which shall ratify this constitution and elect two representatives to the Board shall be considered a member of the Association provided that the Methodists retain a two-third majority on the Board.

Article VI

The Program Committee shall be chaired by the Lake Creek Pastor and shall consist of the pastors of the congregations that are members. They shall arrange the Camp Meeting Program. The District Superintendent shall be a member of this committee.

Article VII

The financial obligations of the organization shall be met by free will offerings taken during the meeting. If such offerings are insufficient to cover expenses, the balance shall be secured by pro-rata assessment, each member church of the organization paying in proportion to the Pastor's Salary.

Article VIII

1. Anyone shall have the right to erect a new camp building on an unoccupied space with the approval of the Camp Meeting Board.
2. When a Camp shall have been vacant for five consecutive years the Board shall have the power to rent same to anyone desiring a camp. The rental fee shall go to the association treasury.

Article IX

The Camp Meeting shall be held annually beginning the first Sunday of August. The Thursday preceding camp meeting shall be designated as clean-up day and in case of rain, the day following (Friday) shall be thus designated. On this day each member of the organization shall be responsible for his proportional share of the work necessary for the cleaning of the camp-grounds.

All Camps should be cleaned by the owners on that day, if possible. All trash and straw shall be burned or removed at least fifty (50) yards from any camp.

Article X

This Constitution shall be effective when the Trustees of the Lake Creek Church have given their consent to it and when it shall have been subscribed by three congregations.

Article XI

This constitution as finally adopted may be amended by a two thirds vote of the members present provided a one year notice of such change has been given.

Voted in Special Joint Session
August 16, 1941

Ratified by the following Methodist Churches: Lake Creek, Smithton, Florence, Stover, Cole Camp, Tipton, Sedalia-Epworth, Windsor, and Pilot Grove.

At the close of the Camp Meeting on August 10, 1975 it was stated that the Constitution was no longer effective and it was voted that the association operate as part of the Lake Creek United Methodist Church with nine Board Members elected by the Annual Church/Charge Conference divided into three classes of three year terms with the provision that one member elected each year must be from another church than Lake Creek. Although the vote was not in accordance with the constitution this was deemed official and this nine member Board has directed the Association since that time.

BIBLIOGRAPHY

Bucke, Emory Stevens, Ed. *History of American Methodism.* Nashville: Abingdon Press, 1964.

Cleveland, Catherine. *The Great Revival in the West: 1797-1805.* Chicago: University of Chicago Press, 1916.

Douglass, Paul F. *The Story of German Methodism*: Cincinnati: Methodist Book Concern, 1939.

Ferguson, Charles A. *Methodists and the Making of America: Organizing to Beat the Devil.* Austin: Eakin Press, 1983.

Harmon, Nolan B. Gen Ed. *The Encyclopedia of World Methodism: A History of the United Methodists and Their Relations.* Nashville: Abingdon Press: 1974.

Kriege, Otto; Becker, Gustuv; Hermann, Matthaus; and Koerner, C.L. *Souvenir of the West German Conference of the Methodist Episcopal Church.* Cincinatti: Jennings and Graham, 1906.

Luccock, Halford; Hutchinson, Paul; and Goodloe, Robert W. *The Story of Methodism.* Nashville: Abingdon Press, 1976.

Johnson, Charles A. *The Frontier Campmeeting: Religious Harvest Time.* Dallas: Southern Methodist University Press, 1955.

Norwood, Frederick A. *The Story of American Methodism.* Nashville: Abingdon Press, 1974.

Sweet, William Warren. *Methodism in American History*, Revised. Nashville: Abingdon Press, 1954.

Sweet, William Warren. *Religion on the American Frontier.* New York, 1964.

Van Ravensway, Charles. *The Arts and Architecture of German Settlements in Missouri: A Survey of a Vanishing Culture.* Columbia: University of Missouri Press, 1977.